Relational Database Programming

A Set-Oriented Approach

Stefan Ardeleanu

Apress®

Relational Database Programming

Stefan Ardeleanu
Bucharest, Romania

ISBN-13 (pbk): 978-1-4842-2079-5　　　　　　　ISBN-13 (electronic): 978-1-4842-2080-1
DOI 10.1007/978-1-4842-2080-1

Library of Congress Control Number: 2016945177

Managing Director: Welmoed Spahr
Lead Editor: Jonathan Gennick
Development Editor: Douglas Pundick
Technical Reviewer: Bradley Beard
Editorial Board: Steve Anglin, Pramila Balen, Aaron Black, Louise Corrigan, Jonathan
    Gennick, Robert Hutchinson, Celestin Suresh John, Nikhil Karkal, James Markham,
    Susan McDermott, Matthew Moodie, Natalie Pao, Ben Renow-Clarke, Gwenan Spearing
Coordinating Editor: Jill Balzano
Copy Editor: Mary Behr
Compositor: SPi Global
Indexer: SPi Global
Artist: SPi Global

Distributed to the book trade worldwide by Springer Science+Business Media New York, 233 Spring Street, 6th Floor, New York, NY 10013. Phone 1-800-SPRINGER, fax (201) 348-4505, e-mail orders-ny@springer-sbm.com, or visit www.springer.com. Apress Media, LLC is a California LLC and the sole member (owner) is Springer Science + Business Media Finance Inc (SSBM Finance Inc). SSBM Finance Inc is a **Delaware** corporation.

For information on translations, please e-mail rights@apress.com, or visit www.apress.com.

Apress and friends of ED books may be purchased in bulk for academic, corporate, or promotional use. eBook versions and licenses are also available for most titles. For more information, reference our Special Bulk Sales–eBook Licensing web page at www.apress.com/bulk-sales.

Any source code or other supplementary material referenced by the author in this text is available to readers at www.apress.com. For detailed information about how to locate your book's source code, go to www.apress.com/source-code/.

Printed on acid-free paper

The application developer … sees himself as a rider on the row.
But the row is not a horse; it's a donkey!

Contents at a Glance

Contents

About the Author

Stefan Ardeleanu was born in Bucharest, Romania, in 1967. He studied math and philosophy, and he was a math teacher for 10 years. Afterwards, he started a career in software development. He was attracted to databases from the beginning, so his entire career in software industry is related to databases and especially to database development and design.

Stefan Ardeleanu is a database specialist, a database architect, and a developer. He has worked in various systems such as Oracle, SQL Server, DB2, and PostgreSQL. He has experience in OLTP, data warehouse, and replication systems.

Stefan is a passionate SQL guy and he has a specific style of development. This style is reflected in his various projects, including replication systems and data migration systems, where this style is highly required.

Stefan is also a database trainer, and he delivers courses in Oracle chain as a partner, especially database development courses and BI courses.

About the Technical Reviewer

Bradley Beard is a software engineer with more than 15 years experience writing dynamic, interactive web sites using ColdFusion and SQL Server. He graduated from Florida Institute of Technology in 2007 with a Master of Science in Computer Information Systems, and studied for his undergraduate degrees in CIS and Technology Management at Herzing University. In 2013, he earned the MCSA: SQL Server 2012 certification from Microsoft, and in 2016, he earned the MCSE: Business Intelligence certification as well.

His continual quest for learning has earned him shelves full of books at home and at work, most of which are about SQL Server, ColdFusion, and general web architectures and frameworks.

He lives in Palm Bay, Florida with his wife, Jessica, and children, Josh, Kaylee, Matthew, and Emma. He also apparently runs an animal shelter made up of his dogs, Lady and Bella, and cats, Spice, Simba, Mercury, and Dobby. He enjoys fishing and spending time with his wife and kids.

Bradley is available for consultation and third-shift remote employment on ColdFusion and SQL Server. Contact him at bradley.beard@gmail.com.

Introduction

I want to share some thoughts from my experiences doing project-based work as an IT contractor. Working as an IT contractor means taking on a mix of short- and long-term projects. In a short-term project, you need to work on a specific task with a team of developers, you need to solve a problem quickly, and then you are done with the project! The team of developers will continue their work and you will search for a new project and challenge.

Three stories...

Some time ago, I was on a project where most of the members were very experienced Java developers. They were developing a document management system that was metadata-based and written almost exclusively in Java. The database was Oracle. The manager and their technical leader invited me to do some Oracle work, to solve some database-specific tasks for the project. All the team members were pure application developers and no one had much expertise with databases. Everything was transformed in SQL, but no one cared too much about that. The developers were good artists and the design was very sophisticated. It was written following the principles of object-oriented programing.

One day, I was in the office listening to some of my colleagues discuss a certain SQL statement. They asked me some questions, which I did not understand. I went over to their desks and looked at what they were working on. I was still confused because the SQL statement in question was quite basic. A self-join was required. I added the self-join and everything worked perfectly well. The team members were amazed! They were not aware that a table can be referenced many times in a join using various aliases. They were not familiar with a self-join!

Later we spoke some more about our careers. They were surprised by the fact that, the same way they spend their entire career doing Java, I spend my entire career doing database development and especially doing SQL. "SQL is so simple. Your task is such a trivial task. Your life is much easier than ours," they said. "We fight with such complicated concepts and you just manipulate rows and columns in your simple query language!"

Another time I was in France with two of my good colleagues, Clark and Marjorie. Clark is American; he has been my manager for a long time and he is a very good friend. Marjorie is an elegant French woman; she is my colleague in support in the French area. We were in a café and we were chatting. We ordered some wine. In addition, I asked for some mineral water. In my country, people mix sparkling water with wine. I thought about asking Marjorie what she thought of this custom, but I knew the answer. To any French person, mixing water with wine is a blasphemy. So I left the water where it was, apart from the glass of wine!

What is the connection between these three shared memories? Being an application developer does not make you SQL independent, in most cases. Whether you like it or not, you will be in contact with SQL, sometimes more or sometimes less! The same way any database developer knows the basics of structured programming, normally most application developers know the basics of SQL. There is no such thing as a superior or inferior language, just useful and compatible ones according to the business. When you are in the country of relational databases, even if you are an application developer, you should learn how to write fair SQL.

Writing Correctly Is Critical to Quality

I believe that one of the most important aspects is the way we write our code, our style of development. It is hard to say what it means to write correctly in the context of software development. There is a degree of subjectivity involved in any judgment of this type. However, I believe that no one can argue with me when I say that the style of development and the way we write our code is proportional with the quality of the software we build.

I am a database developer with many years of experience. During my time spent inside relational databases, I have gathered enough experience to be able to explain that the database area requires a certain and distinct style of development. This is the topic of this book: how to write code inside a relational database in a certain manner, distinct and specific.

There are millions of lines of codes in databases all over the world that are written in a total inadequate manner and these lines of code cause many performance issues in many places. All of these performance issues can be avoided if the programmers understand that a certain style of development is required in a relational database.

The style of this book is not academic although it is a book about database programming. I am a practical person and I think that programming is part of our lives.

Basic Terminology

Due to the direct style of this book and the fact that this book is about database development, which means that it is a technical book, I define some basic terminology. The Internet is full of classifications and manuals, courses and documentation, libraries and practical examples. The concepts are explained and re-explained by specialists. I want to be consistent and to avoid any possible confusion, so let's clarify some concepts and keywords used in this book.

A data-oriented software application is composed of at least one user interface, graphical or not, and the database behind it. When I say database, I am referring mostly to a relational database. One of the main goals for any software application of this type is to allow data access in the database via the user interface. The end users read and write from the database via the user interface. This is what I call a classic data-oriented software system. I will use the term "classic software application" for simplicity. The focus is on the database, so the topic of the software application is the database section.

Another type of data-oriented software application is one that transfers data between classic systems. Medium or large companies have many classic software applications. Every software system of this type has its own purpose, its own database, and will cover

xviii

one part of the business or another. I call this a specific software application. In most cases, there is no user interface and no classic end user. One or many classic systems are the targets and the one or many classic systems are the sources. This system can be a replication system, a data migration system, or an Extract-Transform-Load system (ETL) part of a data warehouse system.

Please be aware of the distinction. One is to develop in a database in a classic system and another one is to develop in a specific system. My main interest in this book is related to the variety of specific systems where many developers work in the same manner they work in classic systems.

Finally, please read Oracle database as Oracle and Microsoft SQL Server as SQL Server.

Types of Software Developers

I am a SQL developer. In other words, I am a classic database developer. For many years, I felt bad about this. I thought that the only pure and authentic database specialists were the database administrators. I wrongly thought that being a database developer, which means a SQL developer, is not a path by itself but a skill among others, an insufficient path that could be associated with something else. People were searching for developers in different combinations like Java plus PL SQL or C# and SQL Server. SQL programming and classic database development was considered an addition to application development. Unfortunately, this is still the case in many places.

Being a software developer means knowing how to develop both the database and non-database layers. Sometimes we must do both and sometimes we do exclusive work.

"He is a very good Java developer, you will see!" "He has many years of experience with C and almost as many with C#. He is a very good programmer!" These kinds of statements are very common. Application developers continue to be the most popular type of developers on the market. For example, developing a web interface is a popular occupation nowadays, and the market is full of good web developers who can satisfy the requirements and build extensive and scalable applications.

What is happening with the database? After the 1990s, the only authentic database people were the database administrators. Being a DBA is a difficult task and involves enormous responsibilities. If something goes wrong in the factory and the inventories fail, the DBA must be there and must find a solution so that the work can continue. It is far from my intention to minimize the role of a DBA: his presence is critical and necessary for any production system. In large enterprises, there are armies of database administrators who take care of the databases.

What about the ones that effectively built the databases as part of the data-oriented software application? For many years, the market neglected them. I admit there is a degree of subjectivism in this statement that I am not afraid to recognize; you can consider it as a personal point of view. The database developers should have received more recognition in the past and even today. Look at the job descriptions in the past, before the BI and data warehouse explosions; you will rarely see explicit requirements for database developers. Happily, today you can see more requests for database specialists; this change is due to the explosion of reporting systems and analytics. For example, an ETL specialist is a highly specialized database developer, and not an ordinary SQL or database developer!

Styles of Development

The same style of development continues to be too often used in both user-interface work and inside the database. Software developers think in patterns of structured and object-oriented programming and apply these principles everywhere in their code, including the databases. Because people don't recognize the database developer as a distinct type of specialist, and because they don't accept a distinct pattern of development for him, databases are often built in an inappropriate style.

Unfortunately, there is still confusion between two different images of the language. I am referring to the confusion between the apparent simplicity of SQL and the potential huge complexity of the written logic with this language. SQL is a paradox. You can learn the basics and understand the language in one week. However, becoming a SQL expert is as difficult as becoming a Java expert.

Software companies want to hire Java or C# programmers with SQL knowledge, and they often consider database programming a secondary skill. The idea of having a distinct style of programming within the database has exists for some years. Happily, this idea is gaining traction. People are starting to see that a database programmer needs to write code differently. I now often see explicit requirements for a database programmer and explicit requests for a non-application developer.

In this book, I want to promote a certain style of development specific to the database. I am referring to SQL development in particular as the most important type of database development. The SQL programmer is critical in a large variety of projects. I want to show that, in the database, a different style of development is required.

Application Developers

I dare to say that, in one way or another, this book is for everyone to a certain degree, and by everyone, of course I am referring to everyone interested in databases, especially in relational databases. This includes business analysts, software testers, all kinds of IT consultants, IT project managers, IT technical leaders, and so on.

Still, this book is especially for programmers, especially application developers like Java, C, C++, C#, and PHP developers. Most of the software today is built on the top of these technologies and on the shoulders of these developers. These developers are focused in their classic languages and they usually work at the user interface level. Many of them are good practitioners of the object-oriented model, for example, and they know how to apply this model to their applications. The object-oriented model is a complex model and it covers many of our realities better than other models.

This book is for the application developer who is asked to work in the database. Very often, moving from the user interface to the database is not seen as a major change and the application developers don't think to adjust anything in the way they write their code.

Some application developers simply ignore any difference; they are not aware of the distinctions because they think that the same model applies to the database. Others judge the SQL language by its apparent simplicity. This book is written especially for application developers who, due to various reasons, subjective or objective, are using the same style of development in the database as the one in the user interface.

Database Developers and Other Audiences

This book is also for those pseudo-database developers who are actually more like application developers and who intensively use the procedural facilities of a language like PL/SQL.

These pages are also for true database developers, SQL developers. It will provide a confirmation of what they are doing right.

This book is for students from IT universities, especially computing and computer science. I hope they will be aware from the beginning that the database is something else and requires a specific style.

This book is for the young programmers who are just starting out in the software industry. I hope they will see that they need to follow a different approach in the database and not develop in the same manner as in the user interface.

This book is also for business people like analysts or testers who deal with data. I believe is good for them to be familiar with the distinctions between the two styles of development.

Finally, this book is for managers and technical leaders of software projects where the database is a critical component. They make the decisions and I hope that some of them will give more importance to the topic of style, for better performance of their software.

The Two Sections of the Book

The book is divided into two large sections. The first four chapters in the book are conceptual. I explain the reason for the two styles of development and justify why we need a different style when we are inside a relational database. I define the concept of the style of development to explain why this is such a critical component for a developer.

Considering that the book is for students, there are sections in the first four chapters where I describe some basic aspects of database development like table design and the characteristics of SQL language. These sections are also required for the sake of my argument but they can be ignored by experienced database developers.

The goal in the first four chapters is to show that a separate style of development is required in a relational database. This style of development is revealed during the book by the opposition with the classic or typical style of development used by most application developers. The style of development that should be used in the database is holistic and set-based as opposed to the atomic and row-oriented style used by many application developers.

The last four chapters of the book are highly practical and are meant to prove the concepts revealed in the first part of the book. I offer a series of examples in two of the most popular database systems: Oracle and SQL Server. These examples illustrate the two styles of development and show the differences. The practices are described and I am not afraid to state that my goal is to promote the holistic and set-based style of development.

■ ■ ■

The Concept of Style

Nowadays, being a programmer is considered a very good career, and more and more people are choosing this path. Like anything in life, writing software code is an activity that is influenced by many factors, both subjective and objective. Many programmers do their work in a certain way according to their experience, knowledge, and preferences. Many embrace a certain style of writing code that is more or less correlated to the application they are creating. Writing a game for children is different than working on a team of developers in an ERP, for example.

As an analogy, I play badminton and my daughter plays tennis. I have my own style in badminton and my daughter has her own style in tennis. If I were to use my badminton style in tennis, I would not do well. To play at an acceptable level, I would need to adapt my style. Even though both are racket sports, there are objective and subjective differences, such as style and rules.

In software development, programmers' specific style of development is composed of the sum of their knowledge derived from both learning process and experiences in various work projects. I consider the style of development a major factor in success for both project teams and developers. Being flexible is essential to good code quality and to a successful career for any programmer.

Style of Development Is Dynamic

I know that I am taking a risk by focusing on a vague concept like *the style of development*. The concept of style is not a scientific notion and it involves a certain degree of subjectivity. I consider the concept of "style of development" similar to the concept of "development approach," but I prefer the terminology "style" because I accept the degree of subjectivity mentioned above.

First, this book is not a scientific one. I am not a scientist. I am a database programmer who has adopted a style of development by working for many years on databases under various systems like Oracle, SQL Server, IBM DB2, and others. I don't claim to reinvent the wheel; in fact, most of the things described in this book should be familiar to many specialists, especially database programmers but not exclusively.

Electronic supplementary material The online version of this chapter (doi:10.1007/978-1-4842-2080-1_1) contains supplementary material, which is available to authorized users.

© Stefan Ardeleanu 2016

S. Ardeleanu, *Relational Database Programming*, DOI 10.1007/978-1-4842-2080-1_1

SQL is such a common language that anyone who says something new about it might be regarded with curiosity and distrust. There are many books and papers on SQL, and many software applications have been written in SQL. SQL is one of the top languages in terms of popularity and usage.

SQL Requires Its Own Style

Therefore, this book is not a book about SQL in the sense that I have something new to say about it. What I want to talk about is the fact that writing SQL code involves a certain style that is somehow distinct from the common styles used in other languages. Even in this area, things have become clearer over the past few years. For example, the set-based approach is now required more often in the software market in many projects. What I want to show is the fact that, in certain situations, software developers should use a certain style of programming. They should use a distinct style of development specific to database programming, not the classic style of structured or object-oriented programming. I am mostly referring to replication systems, data migration systems, Extract-Transform-Load (ETL) systems, or any type of application that moves data between various software systems.

In the theoretical approaches to SQL and in the multitude of courses that have been written, most specialists describe cases where you are supposed to use a certain syntax, and they illustrate the use of SQL via a variety of exercises. They explain that SQL is a query language, so any SQL course is dedicated to the topic of querying. This is the main purpose of SQL: how to get access to data in the relational format.

This is well known. I will focus on another aspect. My thesis is that, when working with a database and using a relational language like SQL, you should adopt a certain style of programming that is not the same as the style you are familiar with as an application developer.

The source of this book is my experience, so you can consider it a practical guide. This is why I prefer to use the rather vague concept of "style of development" instead of a more scientific concept. In my view, this style means the set-based approach but even more than that. The set-based approach that I am promoting here is just the most important characteristic of this style.

I believe that people are becoming more aware of the set-based approach and I see an increased demand for this approach in the market. People are becoming increasingly aware of the need for a certain distinct and specific style of programming in the database area.

Style and Quality

What is the most important thing to everyone involved in a data-oriented software application, apart from the accuracy of information? It's the **performance** of the software itself. There's a big difference between running a data migration interface in one minute and in five minutes! Getting good performance in a database is proportional in many situations to the use of the most appropriate style of development.

Let's continue. The question remains, what is a style of programming?

A Programmer's Own Style

Most programmers have their own style. The way developers write their code is influenced by many factors: their education and background, experience; types of projects, role within projects, their ambition and talent, seriousness, and capacity for organization.

We all know how important it is for programmers to be able to organize their work properly; we all agree that they need to be able to see the details without losing the whole. This is the ideal programmer in an ideal world.

I think of a programmer as similar to a writer. A writer has more or less restrictions than a programmer, depending on how you look at it. Writers are restricted by their audience, and programmers are restricted by their end users and testers. A programmer is sometimes very technical, but a writer may be technical also. The degree of creativity is an essential skill of a programmer, as it is for a writer. However, this degree of creativity is not absolute, as it can be for a writer, but relative because programming is a practical activity and not pure art. Anyway, just as writers have their own style of writing, so programmers have their own style of writing development code.

This is the main topic of this book: I posit that a distinct style of programming is required when writing inside a relational database. I was able to develop this distinct style of development over many years. I think that this style of development is not promoted enough and is not clearly explained in detail. I believe that many IT people will find an advantage to reading this book.

One of my goals is to convince some application developers to reflect upon this proposed style and change something in the way they write when they program databases.

Another goal is related to IT education systems and universities. I think that this style needs to be better promoted in database courses at a university level. Apart from understanding the principles of relational databases, apart from understanding the SQL language, apart from the delivery of specific vendor languages like PL SQL or Transact SQL, it is also very important for the young students to understand how to adapt their code to be more efficient in the database. I do believe this path, the use of a specific **style of development**, should be followed by developers that write code for databases. The best way to make this happen is for it to be explained in universities so the students, the next generation of programmers, will be warned that something needs to change in the way they write when dealing with data.

Common Styles of Development

Now that I have clarified and described the concept of style of development, after admitting that it is a vague concept and not a scientific notion, I will identify some of the major reasons for one style of development or another. Many factors influence a certain style of development. There are schools of development, and these schools are based on certain models and theories. I want to investigate and to describe some of the factors that contribute to a certain style of programming. I will start with a series of questions. These questions are addressed to programmers, especially to application developers.

What type of programmer are you? What is your area of expertise? What programming languages have you used? What paradigm did you follow during your career as a software developer? During your career in the software industry, what was your main path? Were you involved in many levels of development? For example, did you write code at the user interface level and a database level too?

As mentioned, I specialize in database programming and I am a database developer. I was involved at the user interface level during my first years of experience, but I liked databases so much that I decided to specialize in the field of database programming. Are you this kind of programmer? (Not one who necessarily specializes in databases; you may be a highly specialized Java developer, for example.)

Multitasking

Alternatively, you may be a programmer that can do other things too. Maybe you're very flexible; maybe you can switch from PHP or C# to Oracle database and PL SQL, for example. Are you a programmer that performs very well on all types of code, at both the user interface and database level? I have respect for these flexible programmers, as long as they make the distinction and are not trying to work in the same manner in all areas of programming.

Theoretically, when designing and developing an application based on a certain language like C# or Java and using a certain relational database system like SQL Server or Oracle, the application can be written by any kind of IT specialist. In most cases, the programmers can satisfy both goals: they can write code at the user interface level using Java or C# and they can write their logic at the database level using SQL and PL SQL or any other specialized vendor database language.

In most projects, software applications are built by application developers that can write in the database using SQL and associated procedural languages like PL SQL. These developers work on both levels (user interface and database) and they switch from the user interface to the database level periodically. This is the most common situation, with advantages and disadvantages. It is a matter of resources and availabilities, but it is also a matter of skills and costs.

Another approach, which is not so common, is also possible. Specialized database programmers can be used for the database section and application developers can be used for the user interface. Despite the advantages, this is not the general situation; in fact, it's quite rare.

Team Organization

Let's say a company wants to start a new project. It decides to use Java technology and the Oracle database. The managers don't generally search for highly specialized Java developers to allow them to write Java code but forbid them from touching the database under any circumstances! They don't search for specialized database developers to do exclusive database development! Generally managers want to hire people who can do both. In the most common scenario, the expectations are that the developers will be able to write C# or Java code on one hand and write SQL code on the other.

The opposite strategy is not as common, although I have noticed an increase in projects that try to be organized in the opposite manner. I have also noticed an increase in requests for database developers. This growing demand in database development may be explained by a larger number of projects where more specific database expertise is required, like ETL projects and data warehouse projects.

My personal opinion is that the mixed approach will continue to be the most common one. Programmers may prefer the user interface or database, but they are generally able to do both. The question is how are they doing it? Are they doing the job right in both sections? Are they using the same principles of programming in both sections? Or do they use different approaches in different areas?

Any software application is a mirror of a certain business to be implemented. Therefore, the business drives everything, including the database. The programmers can be involved mainly in the current functionalities of the business, the operational systems. For example, they can be involved in classic online transaction processing (OLTP) configurations in classic production systems. Others developers can participate in specific projects like data warehouse, replication systems, or data migration ones. There is a large variety of situations and software applications, and programmers should adapt their capabilities and be flexible. They should write their code in concordance with the specificity of the project.

Apart from classic programming, there is a new type of programming, which is very modern and fancy: visual development. There is a new species of programmer that specializes in tools, most of them visual.

The Visual Experience

A short time ago, I was speaking to some college-bound students. Some of them were considering enrolling in IT universities. I explained some basic facts regarding the world of software developers: the advantages and disadvantages of being a programmer. One of the students told me he wanted to be a programmer without writing a line of code, if possible! His dream was to become a visual developer. I can't imagine a future like this: full of a new type of programmer who has no writing experience and works exclusively with visual tools. Maybe I am too conservative!

So, coming back to the list of interrogations, are you a classic programmer who prefers to write code or are you a visual programmer? This question is reasonable in today's market where the complexity is so high and the number of alternatives is increasing year by year. There are so many technologies, so many languages, and so many visual tools!

These questions are necessary when talking about software programming styles. The purpose of this book is to define and to clarify a **style of programming** specific to the database and to compare it with a classic or typical style. This topic is generally addressed to developers, but not exclusively. A project manager, a technical leader, a tester, a business analyst with technical skills, and a student in an IT university should be interested in this topic too. This book aims to help them understand that changing their style and adapting it to the necessities of the project is in their interest.

Common Models in Programming

The next step in this discussion is the programming model, the general paradigm in which the programmers are bounded or linked. There are several common models and, according to these models, certain programming styles are predominant in the market.

CHAPTER 1 ■ THE CONCEPT OF STYLE

Object-Oriented Programming

The most popular model nowadays is the **object-oriented** paradigm. This model involves a certain style of programming adapted to the principles of object-oriented programming (OOP). This model is one of the most complex. I believe this model is closer to reality than any other. The most common programming languages and frameworks rely on this model, such as Java or C#. All of these languages satisfy the principles of object-oriented programming.

Object-oriented programming is properly described in IT universities all over the world. Young and future programmers become familiar with the model from the very beginning and they understand that most of their activity will be based on this model and paradigm. The principles of object-oriented programming, like encapsulation, polymorphism, data abstraction, and inheritance, are explained both in theory and in practice through a variety of simple applications. Apart from the principles, apart from the model itself, a certain style of programming is promoted automatically. The associated style of programming is, to a certain degree, a consequence of this model and most application programmers start development in a similar fashion and adopt a similar style. This is very normal and rational. The predominant style on the market and a large part of all written software is based in this model and its principles.

Structured Programming

When analyzing the database level and the object-oriented programming model, there are not too many things to discuss. This model has been proven unsuitable for databases, at least for relational ones. The data is too simple and the object-oriented model is too complex. The **relational model** is the one that drives our world of databases! The simplicity of the relational model is obvious compared to the complexity of the object-oriented model. Consequently, the many attempts to convert relational databases to the object-oriented model were unsuccessful. Trying to adapt the object-oriented model and its associated style of programming to the database was one of the reasons for many performance issues in databases in the past!

Apart from the object-oriented paradigm, there is another model that stays closer to the relational model and database programming: the **structured programming model**. Students learn both paradigms and try to understand both models. Later, they decide, depending on the situation and their projects, which model to choose and what associated style of development to adopt. When I say "decide," I don't mean to say they explicitly adopt one style or another. The process of adopting a certain style of programming is a somewhat unconscious process. People generally do not realize this.

In IT universities, while learning **structured programming** students become aware of basic concepts such as variables, structures, arrays, if-else structures, and while loops. They learn how to build a function that returns a void "value." They learn how to create a procedure in certain languages. They become aware of the more modern and complex concepts of class and object, and they learn about data structures, fields, and methods.

Software applications are built following the principles of object-oriented programming or the principles of structured programming. I believe we can consequently accept as programming styles those styles of programming that are in conformity with the principles and models described above, like object-oriented programming or the simpler model of structured programming.

To continue the discussion from another angle, one common characteristic of a good programmer is generality. A good programmer is the one who always tries to be as general as possible in order to handle many situations.

Considering that object-oriented model is the most general and complete programming paradigm, this model can be used as a baseline for any programming activity. Moreover, the style of development that every programmer has is in concordance with the preferred model in most of the cases.

This is generally true but, like any rule and principle, there are exceptions. The database and the relational model are too simple; they're just not compatible with object-oriented programming.

An Alternate Model?

There are situations when object-oriented and structured programming are not convenient. There are certain types of projects in which neither of these two styles are required. Rather, there are situations where these styles should be adjusted to accommodate new features.

It is not hard to guess what kind of scenario I have in mind. What happens if you are developing in a database? Moreover, what should you do if you are instructed to write code in a relational database? What styles of development are the most suitable ones for working within a relational database? These questions drive the content of this book. These are the questions I will answer.

A large part of the businesses that we model (production, sales, supply chain planning or inventory, flight reservation, and others) are implemented in relational databases. Apart from the variety of OLTP systems, there are more and more historical databases such as data warehouses used for analysis and prediction. The associated suite of software applications are built mostly for this data stored in our relational databases. The database is a critical component of the many applications and huge efforts are oriented to these databases.

The two main goals to be achieved are trivial. The databases should have a correct design so the data is stored fairly, and the end users should be able to see the reality of their business. The logic in the databases and in the associated applications should be consistent and accurate so that the performance is acceptable. This mainly means that the response timings should be good.

Considering the importance of the database component, the use of a certain style of development should not be done automatically. Let's consider an example scenario.

Can One Model Fit All?

John Doe is a C# developer. He has spent many years writing C# code and now he needs to build some logic in an Oracle database. He could write his code in a familiar fashion. The object-oriented model is not suitable for the database, so he will use a mixture of structure programming and object-oriented programming, as much as he possibly can. He can't use classes but he can use records or types if he is using PL SQL, etc.

In my opinion, this is one of the biggest issues for many application developers who need to write logic at the database level. They adopt an inappropriate style of development in most cases because they are accustomed to a certain style, to the typical style. They don't analyze the situation and they aren't aware of the different models. They don't realize the necessity of changing something in the way they write their code when they handle the data.

Being a programmer is a vague definition today. People specialize in one language or tool, in one kind of business, in one type of software. There is a large variety of projects and it is difficult to ask someone to know everything.

Starting with Table Design

I know that this section may be seen as inappropriate or too basic by some of my readers. Theoretically, everyone knows what a table is, everyone knows what a column is, and everyone should know what a constraint is! Still, considering the large audience of this book, I would like to describe some of the basic considerations regarding table design. Feel free to skip this section or read it quickly.

As mentioned, I am discussing how people should write their code inside a relational database. Imagine that you are part of a team of programmers starting development. You are already familiar with the two models, the object-oriented model and the structured model, and you know the SQL language. The relational database can be anything. It can be Oracle, SQL Server, DB2, or PostgreSQL.

I think that database development starts with the design. This is why I included this section, because this is the starting point in your development activity. So let's review some basics.

There is a list of object types (nothing to do with object-oriented programming) in any database, and among various classifications of these types, one is the most important. We can classify objects as **base objects** and **procedural objects**. The developer is obviously involved mainly in the set of procedural objects. However, despite any appearances, development actually starts from the design of the base objects. To be more specific, development starts from the **table design**. A good developer should know this and not undermine its importance.

The Table as an Entity

The database is firstly the sum of its tables, and the table is the center of the universe in the universe of databases. I am referring to relational databases. Efficient database development means, firstly, the proper design of the tables. The table design starts from the business, like anything else in software development. The table is the mirror of the business, in the sense that the useful business information is stored in the tables.

The database developer needs to be aware of the meanings of the tables. The table design can be implemented by specialized architects, by business analysts, or by developers, but the developers need to have a good understanding of it. The set of procedural code they will write has one single purpose: to get everything from those tables.

What does "the table design" mean? This is an elementary question. The table is a combination of **columns** and **rows**, like an Excel file. There are two ways of looking at a table: the design view and the execution view. In the design view, you can see the definition of the table and the columns. In the execution view, you can see the data, you can see the rows, and you can analyze and understand the data.

Let's talk about the design view, the table definition. This simply means the set of columns that make up the table; the columns in the table correspond to the characteristics of that something that needs to be defined.

The Table As A Sum of Columns

Each column should have a **name**, unique for a specific table. The name cannot exceed a certain length, according to the database system. The column should have a certain **data type**, from the available list of data types for each database system. The most important data types are string, numeric, and data, with variations and subtypes. The column can be a **business** column, with a clear business meaning, like the first name of the student. The column can be a **technical** or **artificial** column, used for implementing the consistency of data, like an **identifier**, such as a student id. This column has no meaning by itself and the end user will not understand anything from it. However, these columns are very important for the developers and they manipulate these artificial columns with priority.

The table designers define the columns. They specify the relevant names and they associate the correct data types according to the business requirements. The first stage of development, the table design, ends with the layer of **constraints,** a critical aspect of the design but also part of the first layer of database development. The designers, who sometimes are the developers, should be able to use this facility and define all the constraints correctly.

Database Constraints

The following are the most common types of constraints. Various database systems may have them all or not.

- The first type of constraint is the so-called **NOT NULL**. A column can have such importance that should always be filled with something when data is added into the table. For example, the name of a student is essential. What is the relevance of a student if we do not know the name! This column will be defined as mandatory. This means that whenever you add a new student, the name should be specified; otherwise an error will be raised by the system and the student cannot be added. Adding the **NOT NULL** constraint whenever possible is a very good practice. However, having fewer null values is better for the development because many problems are caused by the null values in logic!

- Maybe the most important type of constraint is the **primary key**. One of the principles of a relational database is the fact that you identify one **row** in a table. The identification should be unique. Normally, good design means not accepting tables without a primary key. Every table should have a primary key, at least in a normalized database. The developer should always be aware of the primary keys and will manipulate them later during her development activity. There is one primary key per table.

The primary key can be an artificial column or not, but I recommend the use of artificial columns whenever possible. This kind of column has no meaning apart from its role, which in this case is to identify one row in a table. Still, the primary key constraint can be defined on a business column, like social security number, but it is not a common practice. The primary key can also be defined for a combination of columns. If you want to define the constraint for a pair of columns, the combination of columns should be unique.

- A similar type of constraint is the so-called **unique** constraint. This constraint is similar to the primary key, in the sense of the uniqueness of the column, or pair of columns. However, there is a difference in the meaning. The purpose of the primary key is to identify a row in a table. The purpose is highly artificial. By contrast, the unique constraint is generally a business constraint, specifying that a certain column should be unique due to the business requirements. For example, a social security number is not the perfect column for a primary key, although you can use it if you really want to. However, it is a perfect column for a unique constraint. Compared to a primary key, which is one per table, many unique constraints per table are generally accepted. The unique constraint can also be defined for a combination of columns, which means that a combination of columns should be unique. The perfect combination, in my opinion, is to have an artificial primary key and a business unique key, if it exists.

- A more complex type of constraint is the **check** constraint. This is a simple formula that should be applied to one column in the table and it implements simple rules. The most common one is the affiliation to a list of values, like gender, that can be either Male or Female. Generally, but not always, a check constraint can be combined with a **NOT NULL** constraint. Combining check and **NOT NULL** is very important because doing so covers all situations for that column and leaves nothing out. Although the table stage is when you prepare for development, it's a good idea to have the logic in your mind, the set of procedures and functions that will follow.

- The **foreign key** constraint allows you be sure that when you separate distinct pieces of information, they will remain consistent. Normally, every table has a primary key, so it is uniquely identified by that primary key. Every table should store the distinct type of information in a transactional and normalized system. The tables are related by foreign keys and are the base for most of the **joins** in the logic. Understanding and properly defining foreign keys is a critical step and the set of foreign keys is the key to understanding the joins that are to be found everywhere in the logic that will follow.

- The last type of constraint is the **default** constraint. This is not seen as a constraint by all systems. It is not actually a constraint because it does not restrict the column in any way. This is just a default value that is added in the absence of an explicit value. For example, most of the students in university in Paris are from Paris; let's say 80%. In this case, whenever adding a new student, based on the probability of that student being from Paris, the locality can be skipped at insert time and the default value, Paris, can be added automatically.

This set of constraints is the first layer of consistency of the data within the database. A programmer who is working within the database needs to be aware of this layer. This is not part of the logic itself, our topic of discussion, but it can be considered as such.

For example, the gender is checked by the values Male and Female. This can be done in a stored procedure without any problems but why would you do it? The programmer can have an error handling procedure, which catches the error identifier and the error message, detects the name of the constraint that was violated, identifies the table and column, and raises an intelligible message. However, the rule itself is checked by the database layer, the first layer of constraints.

The programmers write the logic but they need to be aware that this already started in the layer of table design and constraints. The logic is generally for the data, and the data is defined in tables, and the developers will continuously manipulate these tables. The potential data should be carefully analyzed; the business should be explained by those with deep knowledge of the data. Based on this information, when designing the tables, the programmer will start the development process by implementing a correct table design including the layer of constraints.

One important matter about the constraints is their names. It is a very good practice to give explicit names that are relevant in terms of business. Don't forget that the constraint names are visible in error messages. When you see the message, if the name is explicit and relevant, you will understand right away what it is about and you can quickly identify the starting point for the investigation. Also, you can easily find the objects in the metadata associated with every database: this is also an important matter.

What Developers Must Know

Now let's come back to the application developers who are thrown into the middle of a database! What if these application developers are not familiar with the database and they don't know too much about tables and columns? Although not very common, it could happen. They know what a variable is; they know what a data type is; they know to associate a data type with a variable; they know to specify a name to the variable; and they know that the name cannot exceed a certain length. They are also familiar with the Excel file! They can easily translate everything and have a basic understanding; they have a starting point.

So, what they need to know first when dealing with the database development is not the logic itself; they already know the principles of structured programming so they have a good background. They firstly need to become familiar with the basic objects, with the tables. The table is the object type that will be accessed in the logic almost everywhere.

See Listing 1-1. You will create a table and you will add a variety of constraints to enforce the rules described earlier for the columns.

Listing 1-1. Design of a Table

```
CREATE TABLE Students
(
        Student_Id INT NOT NULL,
        Student_Name VARCHAR (30) NOT NULL,
        SSN VARCHAR (30) NOT NULL,
        Locality_Id INT,
        Birth_Date DATE,
        Gender VARCHAR (10) NOT NULL
);
ALTER TABLE Students ADD CONSTRAINT  PK_Students_Student_Id
PRIMARY KEY (Student_Id);
ALTER TABLE Students ADD CONSTRAINT  UQ_Students_SSN
UNIQUE (Student_Id);
ALTER TABLE Students ADD CONSTRAINT  CK_Students_Gender
CHECK (Gender IN ('Male', 'Female'));
ALTER TABLE Students ADD CONSTRAINT  FK_Students_Localities
FOREIGN KEY (Locality_Id)REFERENCES Localities (Locality_Id);
```

Listing 1-1 illustrates the above considerations. You can see the primary key, an artificial column named Student_Id with no business meaning and with the simple goal of identifying one row in the table, the uniquely identified student. In this way, you can be sure that you can read and write a certain student, without any doubts. You can also see the column Student_Name, a descriptive field but mandatory, a column with a clear business meaning. Let's look at the column SSN; the social security number is a business column that holds the attribute of uniqueness. This is the business key of the table and a unique constraint was defined for this column. The column Gender is a column with a very low selectivity (only two possible values: Male and Female). A **check** constraint was applied to the column so you know that no other value can be specified for this column. The locality is referenced by the **foreign key** constraint. The tables are linked by relations and these relations are implemented and **checked** in most cases by the mechanism of foreign keys. Assume that you already built another table with the localities; another primary key that is referenced in the students table will identify one locality.

The table design, without being pure development of any type, can be considered as such for someone working in the database. A developer who is not aware of this can't develop properly in any database.

Let's Begin Coding

Listing 1-1 is extremely simple. These basic considerations are very familiar to most programmers that work with data. The goal of this book is not to describe SQL but to promote a development style. Still, an introduction to relational databases and the SQL language is required.

I started with the table definition and I illustrated the most common set of constraints attached to the tables. I illustrated a set of data definition language.

In the relational database, there are various classifications. As you saw earlier, there are base objects and procedural objects. The table is the base object by definition, the most important one. In the relational database, everything is for, against, and with the tables. This is why a programmer should firstly understand this simple object. You are in the relational database and you handle tables! You look into the relational database: you are looking at the tables! It is much simpler than what you already know; all you need is to be open and try a paradigm shift.

The first task for the programmer is to understand the table. Rows and columns; it's too simple! Surprisingly, sometimes even simplicity is a problem. Instead of experiencing satisfaction, some developers complain about the simplicity of the model.

Someone might say that all these considerations I've talked about have nothing to do with development; they are work for a DBA. I disagree completely. I think that a database developer should understand the table design better than the DBA! The DBA's generally do not care too much about meanings. They are administrators; they have a very important role. However, the DBA's do not know the business well because they are not experts of that type. The database developers know it much better. Some books say that the DBA creates the tables. Actually, the table creation is part of the database developer's responsibilities. The DBA builds the appropriate scripts for the production environment, but the tables were created by the developer in the development environment a long time ago! The DBAs are aware of the table design because they manage the system, especially production. Still, the true creators of the tables are the database developers because they know the meanings, they build the logic, and they know the purpose of each column because they will manipulate them in the logic later during the development process.

The database developer is the one that handles the logic within the database. In many applications, the complexity of the logic within the database is extremely high. This complexity can be handled in many ways. Having application developers working in an inappropriate style in the database will harm the database infinitely even more than a lack of indexes, for example. The application developer should understand the principles of database development when writing code in the database.

Revisiting the Example

Let's start the database development; let's start writing code into the database. For that, we'll examine the responsibilities of a database developer. The following are some examples:

- The programmer builds the logic that allows data access.

- The programmer builds the logic that allows end users to read the data and to write the data.

- The programmer may build the mechanisms that transfer the data between various databases.

- The programmer may build, for example, an ETL, a replication system, or a data migration system. In each case, they are responsible for the data transfer between various systems.

These are just some examples of tasks a programmer may have. There are various situations and I will analyze some of them later. The programmer can be a database developer or an application developer who is doing database development along with application development.

The programmers should be aware of the tables. They can design them or not, but they definitely use them all the time so they need to know them very well. Regarding the set of constraints like primary key, check, **NOT NULL**, unique and foreign keys, a good and fair implementation is a key to successful development. More than that, a correct design of the constraints is part of the primary development.

Everything starts with the table design. Let's see one example of good design wrongly implemented. I will show you how a good table design may lead to a nightmare in future development if it is not properly understood. Let's say you have an important entity in an application, like an invoice. You have an invoice number and an invoice identifier, an artificial primary key. This is the header. In the invoice detail, you have a combined primary key between the invoice identifier from the header and a current number. See the design in Listing 1-2.

Listing 1-2. Design Is Just the First Step

```
CREATE TABLE Invoices
(
    Invoice_Id INT NOT NULL,
    Supplier_Id INT NOT NULL,
    Invoice_Date DATE NOT NULL,
    CONSTRAINT  PK_Invoices_Invoice_Id
PRIMARY KEY (Invoice_Id)
);
ALTER TABLE Invoices ADD CONSTRAINT  FK_Invoices_Suppliers
FOREIGN KEY (Supplier_Id) REFERENCES Suppliers (Supplier_Id);
CREATE TABLE Invoices_Details
(
    Invoice_Id INT NOT NULL,
    Current_Number INT NOT NULL,
    Quantity INT NOT NULL,
    Currency VARCHAR (30) NOT NULL,
    CONSTRAINT  PK_Invoices_Details
PRIMARY KEY (Invoice_Id, Current_Number),
        CONSTRAINT  FK_Invoices_Invoices_Details
FOREIGN KEY (Invoice_Id)
        REFERENCES Invoices (Invoice_Id)
);
```

Good Design May Be Wrongly Implemented

Listing 1-2 is an example of a good design. Still, if implemented incorrectly, it may have bad consequences. Imagine that the column Current_Number is a volatile column; every time new details are added to the invoice, the values are recreated based on certain criteria like a true current number. For example, let's assume that the details are shown and the current number is ordered by quantity. In this case, the first detail today will become the third one tomorrow! Imagine that the details need to be updated. Very often, an update is done based on the primary key. In the given conditions, this is impossible. Another field needs to be added to satisfy the condition of uniqueness. This is true if the mechanism of the current number cannot be changed. Alternatively, the current number will not be recreated but kept with every change in the invoice.

It is critical for the primary key to be set correctly because very often this is the criteria for an update. If you want to **update** anything, you need to be able to **identify** it first. The primary key should not just be unique but also **stable**. The **stability** needs to be combined with **uniqueness** for the primary key to indeed be the criteria for row identification and, consequently, for an update. Otherwise, you need to use something else, maybe a business unique constraint, for the update.

Imagine you have to service a part of an invoice with the current number 12. The invoice id is 100. Therefore, the pair 100, 12 identifies this invoice detail. If you want to update something in this detail, first you query the detail based on the pair 100 and 12, and then you update. If the current number is volatile, tomorrow it will become 20. The pair will become 100, 20 instead of 100 and 12. Trying to update the pair 100 and 12 will update another detail. Therefore, this is a good design but it hasn't been correctly implemented by the application developer. The primary key should be unique and mandatory. More than that, if the primary key is the criteria for update, it needs to be stable.

Stability is another component of a primary key and this is something that the developer needs to be aware of. Most of the developer's work is on these tables, trying to populate them with data. This is the reason why understanding the tables and the associated constraints is critical.

Now you can see how the software programmer is already involved in the logic even before starting it. Later the developers will receive some tasks to update the details of the invoice. They will need to make a huge effort because someone did not understand the table design. The combination of the invoice number and the current number is unique. This pair will identify one row in a table. Still, the primary key is not stable because the current number is volatile. The primary key is not persistent. The current number changes all the time after the table is updated, and the developers are forced to find other ways to identify the rows. They need to define and populate another artificial column to solve the problem. They should add a unique business constraint, but that one is still artificial. If they were involved in the table design from the beginning and possessed the proper knowledge, they could have avoided all of these issues.

This is why I don't agree that the DBA is responsible for the design of the base objects like tables. The DBA is responsible for the implementation in production (eventually adding partitions and indexes, and using parallelism) but the design itself is the responsibility of the database developer.

Are You Ready for SQL?

I just clarified the concept of table as the most important one for a database programmer or an application programmer dealing with data. The tables are related to each other by logical relations enforced by the first layer of constraints.

You have a database; you have a variety of tables. You want to access these tables, to populate and read the contents of the tables. What are you using? You may be a true database developer, or you may be a Java or C developer. Perhaps you are used to dealing with systems in the classic way and you need to handle data in a relational database. You can use any database system like Oracle, SQL Server, MySQL, or PostgreSQL. Maybe you are in the middle of a specialized data warehouse that is using Teradata and you need to work in an ETL interface system. Well, there's good news. There is a standard, as you know.

SQL is the standard and most relational database systems use it. Yes, this standard is implemented differently in different systems, and there are differences between syntaxes, but the differences are minor. Dealing with one database system and switching into another database system is relatively easy. As you know, every database system has its own programming language, which is an extension of SQL. Oracle has the PL SQL language; SQL Server uses Transact SQL language and others. However, the SQL is almost the same. All of the software suppliers realize the advantages of having a standard and they adapted the syntaxes to be compliant with it.

This is one reason to why being a database developer means first being a SQL developer. The existence of the standard makes it easy for database developers to switch from one database system to another. You will see more on that soon.

SQL is one of the most popular languages nowadays after so many years of usage. Still, the number of true and good SQL developers is not very high.

There are PL SQL developers. There are people who say that they work exclusively in Oracle database as developers. Alternatively, there are exclusive Transact SQL developers. This is absurd, in my opinion. I believe that they are mainly SQL developers. A true database developer is mostly a SQL developer. Most of her work is pure SQL. Learning new syntaxes to create a stored procedure in Oracle or SQL Server is not a big deal! The transition from one system to another is very simple. The principles of structured programming apply to all of these dedicated database-programming languages.

Now it is time to see what SQL actually is. The review will be basic because I consider this quite common and the topic of the book is not to describe the SQL language.

■ ■ ■

CHAPTER 2

SQL: Beauty and the Beast

In the first chapter, I analyzed the table design, including the layer of constraints, and I concluded that this is actually the beginning of the development process. Database development includes database design and we cannot analyze one without the other.

Let's continue with the next step!

When we speak about development, we should speak about a language. Any classic development activity requires a language. Do we have a language? The answer is obvious, yes, and that language has been available for many years; it is the universal language for relational databases. The surprise is the fact that this language is not a typical programming language. This language is a **query** language. It is the **SQL** language, often knows as the popular **Structured Query Language**.

This may be shocking to some people. The topic of this book is the necessity of a certain **style of programming** inside a database. So we are thinking, obviously, of a classic programming language. It comes as a big surprise that we are discussing something else! We are talking about a query language and not about a classic programming language! This may seems unusual to anyone not familiar with databases.

Can a Query Language Be So Important?

In a data-oriented software application there are many people involved in the generic activity of **query**. Customer support people, business analysts, consultants, testers, and QA analysts all query the data regularly to get whatever they need. They are not doing any programming; they are simply querying. Almost everyone is querying the data in a certain way, and almost all of them use SQL for that purpose. SQL is not a dedicated language for programmers. SQL is a language for every category of people who, for some reason or another, need access to data. There are so many non-programmers working at software companies with a good level of SQL! This shows once more that SQL is something other than a classic programming language; it is very close to a natural language.

Databases Require a Language

A database requires a query language in order to access the data inside it. This applies to any kind of database. As mentioned, this query language is not necessarily a programming language in the classic sense. This query language can be embedded in

© Stefan Ardeleanu 2016
S. Ardeleanu, *Relational Database Programming*, DOI 10.1007/978-1-4842-2080-1_2

a programming language and used by database programmers, or it can be used for the simple purpose of data access. A good programmer working inside a database should have at least an acceptable knowledge of the query language.

A parallel with old times comes to my mind. At one time, Latin was the only academic language and all the others were considered barbarian languages. All books were written in Latin for many centuries. Today, some programmers consider a classic programming language to be like Latin and they consider SQL, for example, to be a barbarian language. They say, for example, that since SQL is not a dedicated language according to their criteria of evaluation and according to their experience in all sort of standard classic programming languages like Java, C# or anything else, it must be a primitive and barbarian language. I feel that this is an arrogant and irrational vision. I strongly disagree with it, as we all should.

SQL Is a Useful Language

The software development world is a very practical world. The quality of a language consists firstly in its utility. More than that, the utility should be associated with simplicity. SQL is a very useful language, and the fact that it is used by so many categories of professionals, not just by programmers, is an advantage, not a disadvantage. The fact that non-programmers can learn it proves that SQL is a good language, and it may be used as a query language by almost everyone in the enterprise.

Moreover, programmers, even specialized database developers and other kinds of developers doing work inside a database, use SQL as part of a programming language in their activity of database development.

Programmers Must Adapt

When dealing with data in a relational format, there are some basic things to do. First, you need to understand the concept of a table, a row, and a column. You need to understand the table design and its constraints. Second, you need to understand and use the associated query language specific to data access in that format.

This is the first paradox for application developers who wants to do database work. They know classic programming and now they need to become familiar with another type of language, one that is much simpler than what they already know, and, more importantly, a different language than what they are accustomed to: a query language. This can be confusing, at least in the beginning.

The application developer needs to understand that a query language is required due to the nature of data. This is a very basic and trivial statement. The data exists to be read and written. We need a way to access the data within our databases. This is the definition of a query language; it allows data access, read and write. More than that, it allows metadata access, both read and write.

This is one difference between the two levels: user interface level versus the database level. The goal in the database is specific and particular: data and metadata access. From the beginning, the expectations are clear. There are the expectations of a reader, and the expectations of a writer, all in a certain format. At the user interface level, we can theoretically and potentially expect anything. At the database layer, we have one main expectation and we want only one thing. I am sure you know very well what that is!

A Different Style Is Needed

The presence of a query language is one indication of the necessity for a certain style distinct from the one used at the user interface level, where the style is driven mainly by the general models mentioned in Chapter 1. In the database, the required style should be conform to the particular expectations and goals described above. The style of development should be somehow associated with the goal: see the data, get the data, write the data, change the data, delete the data, and move the data. Since the goal is straightforward and simple, so the style should be. There is no need for the complexity you see at the user interface level.

The fact that the query language is a natural language and the basics can be learned in one or two weeks is terrific. From what I know about programming, **simple things are better things**. To me, the simplicity and naturalness of the query language is a big advantage for everyone, including application developers who deal with the database, and students learning how to write software code.

Nevertheless, some application developers prefer to make things more complicated because they believe they have some artistic visions in terms of programming. I agree with the idea that a programmer is an artist, but always a practical one. The programmer has some clear goals and these goals are driven by the business. The programmer is not the absolute leader of their work, as the artist is.

So the first thing application developers should do, if they are really involved in database programming, is to forget for a while about their classic programming background and dedicate some time to understanding a simple but vital language for their work. They need to spend some time learning SQL. They also need to comprehend the importance of a query language in their programming activity and they need to understand that a query language is something vital for their software development activity. They should not complain about the lack of aesthetics, for example, when speaking about SQL. You cannot compare apples and pears.

Even in the absence of SQL and not referring explicitly to the relational database, but speaking about any database, it comes down to basics. The data is for being queried, and this activity is critical when implementing the logic inside the database. Therefore, the query language (because there should be a query language, either SQL or something else) is critical for the development process. Even theoretically, we may say that the query language should be integrated in the development process and the style of development is influenced by the query language.

Understanding What SQL Is and Is Not

Considering the extended audience of this book, including students and application programmers with limited experience in the field of databases, let's switch from the complex considerations described above to the common description of the SQL language that will follow in the next pages.

SQL Is Not Classical Programming

Let's analyze the query language. The relational model of data is trivial: tables, rows, and columns. For such a basic model, there is a trivial language. This language is a dedicated, specific language for accessing rows and columns in almost any possible way.

SQL is a query language and a standard that is followed closely by almost all of the vendors that build database systems.

As a query language, SQL is a set of instructions with a clear purpose: to allow data and metadata access. SQL is English-like, and the statements are very natural and intuitive. The keywords are so common that you don't need to think too much to understand how to use them.

Learning SQL is easy. Still, to become a good SQL professional, you need to spend some years on the subject.

As application developers, we always need to be aware that SQL is **different** in its nature. I have had discussions with Java, C#, and web programmers and they have told me that SQL should not be integrated in their philosophy of programming. They don't consider the SQL language as programming at all. Actually, they are right. SQL is indeed very different. More than that, SQL is not a classic programming language, according to their standards. It is true that you cannot compare SQL to C# or Java. SQL has a different nature and it is obviously something else. SQL is firstly a query language and any comparison is completely inappropriate. SQL by itself is a separate language, apart from any other classic programming languages.

SQL Is About Querying

Now, since I've clarified what SQL is not (an unusual start for a definition but recommended here due to some basic misunderstandings) let's see what SQL is. I will start with the three words: structured query language:

1. **SQL is a language**. Surprisingly or not, SQL is apparently not a strong formalized language because it is more like a **natural** language. The main keywords it uses are common words, like select, insert, and delete. Being a natural language is one major reason why SQL is available to a large variety of people, not just programmers and technical people. Many non-programmers use it at various levels depending on their skill and interest.

2. **SQL is a query language** as part of a classic programming language like PL SQL, for example. The purpose of SQL is to query the data and metadata. By querying the data, I mean both read and write processes.

3. **SQL is a structured language**. This means that SQL is organized in a way that reminds us of one of the models, the structured model of programming. The principles of structured programming are satisfied in this query language to a certain extent, and this is one reason why some programmers say that the use of SQL is based on the use of structured programming. To some extent, this is true. I will explain more about this later. There are differences and they come from the nature of SQL, from the nature of the data.

A query language has a different and particular scope. Querying something is a particular task and, considering this limited goal, we can understand the essence of SQL language.

Components of the SQL Language

When we analyze a data-oriented software application, such as an inventory system or a software application for a hospital or university, we see similar components. The purpose is to populate the database via a user interface, either web-based or desktop-based. It consists of a user interface and the corresponding database in the back end. In most cases, one of the main goals is to populate the database with information and to access this information. The end users access the data in the database via the user interface. These goals, of reading and writing data in the database, are achieved by the use of SQL. By data, I obviously mean business data, like invoices, inventory, or patient information.

As you know, the data is written in tables. Apart from this well-known task of reading and writing the data, SQL is responsible for another task. The data within the database can be classified in two categories. A database stores **data** and **metadata**. For example, whenever a table is created, metadata information is written in the database automatically. Any database system has a set of tables, called system tables or data dictionary, and these contains information about the business objects. When a table is created, the information that defines the table, like the name of the table, the names of the columns, the data types for the columns, the constraint information, and all the design characteristics of the table, is written in the set of system tables.

This type of information is named **metadata** information, which means data about data. Therefore, when writing with SQL in a relational database, we understand either writing data or writing metadata, and similarly when reading, we can read any of two types of data. These considerations are useful and allow me to continue to show the most important characteristics of SQL, the bread of any database developer and the bread of any application developer that writes code in the relational database.

There are several sections of statements, all of them described in any SQL course. Learning SQL means learning and understanding these statements. This is very easy; everyone can learn them. Then the hard part follows: you need to start the process of understanding the data. My tip to you: start becoming friends with the data. This task may take years!

The SQL language is composed mainly of four sections of instructions, called sublanguages or subsets of the SQL language. The sections are the followings:

1. The first sublanguage is the data manipulation language (**DML**). This subsection of SQL is the section responsible for **data access**, in both ways as active and passive, by read and write. Any instruction that relates to reading the data or writing the data is part of DML.

2. The second sublanguage is the data definition language (**DDL**). This is the section of SQL responsible for **metadata access**. Creating new objects, like tables but also any type of object in a database, is an action that generates metadata in the system. When create a table or a view, many rows are added in the metadata responsible for tables and views.

3. An additional sublanguage is the data control language (**DCL**). This section of the language handles the security within the database like assigning privileges, for example. Various objects can be accessible to users and privileges are given to them. The most common instructions are **grant** and **revoke**.

4. The last of the main sections is the transaction control language (**TCL**). This section allows us to control the transactions, and this is a critical section for a developer. The transaction is a critical concept and the developer should have a perfect understanding of the transaction. At the database level, inside the database logic, one of the most difficult tasks is having consistent control of transactions. The commit and rollback statements are critical in any database logic.

All of these sections contain specific statements. This limited set of statements is almost everything you need to know; you can say that this is the SQL language! The first section is the most important one for a developer. Most of the database development code is composed from DML statements; maybe 90% of the code written by a programmer within the database is composed of these instructions.

Queries and Clauses

If you pick any SQL course and divide it in half, you can see that the first part is dedicated to this type of statement. The QUERY is a statement dedicated to reading data (or metadata) of any kind. QUERY in this case is the passive process of reading. This is the most important thing for anyone working at the database level. The purpose of reading is the most elementary and critical goal for anyone dealing with data. The simplicity and the difficulty of SQL is the QUERY; being able to select the data properly is an essential skill for a good database professional, especially a database developer or data analyst.

Most SQL statements can be divided into a subset of phrases called clauses. A **clause** is a part of a SQL statement. A "select" statement contains several possible clauses.

1. The first clause is always the **SELECT** clause. In the select clause of a query, you specify which columns or expressions you want to visualize. An expression can be anything: any combination of various columns and constants plus SQL operators like addition and concatenation. The columns or expressions are separated by a comma. This is always the first clause in a query.

2. The second part of the statement is always the **FROM** clause. In this clause, you specify the source(s) of data. You need to mention the list of tables from where you will get the columns and expressions in the select clause. The list of tables or views should be valid objects in the database.

3. Next is the **WHERE** clause. In this section, you specify
    the criteria for the data and the conditions that need to
    be satisfied. For example, if you want to see the students
    from Paris, you add criteria for the locality to be Paris. The
    conditions are separated by logical operators like conjunction
    or disjunction. Be aware of the distinction between the SQL
    logic and the classic logic. The SQL logic is a different type of
    logic. In this logic, there is another choice apart from true and
    false: null. Null means the lack of any value.

4. If there are groupings, two additional clauses are required.
    The first clause is **GROUP BY**. If the data needs to be grouped
    by certain columns or expressions, you use this clause. For
    example, if you want a list of teachers and the numbers of
    courses taught by each teacher, you can group by the teacher
    and count the courses.

5. If you have another level of filtering, at the level of groups, a
    new clause is required. This is the **HAVING** clause. This clause
    allows you to filter at the level of groups. The **HAVING** clause
    is correlated with the **GROUP BY** clause.

6. If the data should be ordered, the **ORDER BY** clause is
    required. This clause allows you to sort the data according to
    the columns or expressions that you want to sort.

The queries (SQL SELECT statements) and their clauses are maybe the most
important ones for a developer dealing with database programming; they are the simplest
ones and the more complicated ones at the same time. Getting the data is simple enough,
theoretically, but it can become very complicated, which happens very often because the
business itself can be very complicated.

The first thing you need to know, when dealing with data, is how to query data properly.

Inserting, Updating, and Deleting

The rest of the DML contains the instructions for writing the data. There is one type
of instruction per possible write operation. The insert statement is for adding new
information, the update statement is for editing information, and the delete statement is
for deleting data in the database.

All these statements are well known, in theory and in practice. What is important is
that all of these statements are somehow related to the select statement, to the query.
In almost all cases, in order to be able to write something, you need to be able to read.

- **You want to insert something**. If you want to add some new
  data manually, you should specify the values one by one for each
  column; this is relatively simple. However, if you want to add
  some data into a destination from a source of data, you first need
  to be able to identify the source of data. In addition, that source of
  data can be a simple or a very complicated query. There are two

main types of insert statements. The **INSERT VALUES** statement, which means manually, specifies the values to be added for each column, and one value will be inserted at a time. This is very straightforward. Then there it is the **INSERT SELECT** statement, which means inserting the data into a destination from a source of data. The source of data can be trivial or can be a complicated query. The degree of complexity can vary from infinite simplicity to infinite complexity. This is another example of how SQL can be extremely simple and extremely complicated in various situations.

- **You want to update something**. Update statements can also be very simple or very complicated. An **UPDATE** means changing some values in some columns or rows according to the business requirements. The update statement can be divided into two phases. First, you need to execute a select statement and identify the rows to be updated. Second, you need to identify the new values because, in an update statement, you update certain rows and you add new values for the columns you want to change. To identify the new values, you can specify some manual values or you can get the new values from subqueries. An update can occur from several sources of data, and identifying these sources can be trivial or difficult. An update can be extremely complicated; you may spend hours until you get it right!

- **You want to delete something**. The **DELETE** statement can also be elementary or complex. Compared to an update, things are simpler because you have only one problem here: identifying the rows to be deleted. You do not have any new values because you are simply deleting some data. Still, identifying the rows to be deleted can become a difficult task depending on the requirements, or it can be a trivial matter.

To conclude, the general concept of querying data can mean either reading or writing and reading data. Reading data means the effective query, the **SELECT** statement. Writing data means one of the three actions, **INSERT**, **UPDATE,** or **DELETE**. These are the main types of tasks for a database developer. This activity should be incorporated into the programmer agenda and the programmer should adjust his style of development according to the task.

What About Programming?

Until now, the discussion has been centered on the language as a **query** language. The topic of this book is the style of a programmer, the way he should write software code. Moreover, the discussion has been about SQL, mainly a query language! But what about classes, objects, entities, arrays, and structures? I have not mentioned any of these programming concepts!

As you know, most vendors developed their own true database programming languages, apart from the query language. Oracle's programming language is called

PL/SQL. Microsoft developed the Transact-SQL programming language for SQL Server. IBM developed its own programming language for DB2 named SQL PL. In other words, many vendors offer a private, proprietary programming language for their databases.

All of these languages are structured programming languages and they satisfy the principles of **structured** programming. Any beginner studying PL/SQL or a similar offering will learn, to a certain degree, similar things and features as in a typical, non-database-oriented structured programming language. Any beginner will start with the basics. He will learn what a variable is and how to use it, and he will learn about data types. He will study how to use conditional statements, loops, if-else statements; he will learn to handle exceptions.

A very important feature of a procedural language, specific to databases, is the **cursor**. The cursor is a great feature because it allows us, in combination with loops, to move inside a data set from one row to another to perform various manipulations. The application developer is often happy to discover the cursor facility, and he learns how to use this feature easily and right away. Unfortunately, this feature is used in excess and is a reason for many performance issues in the databases.

■ **Note**   You will see later how cursors used in excess can lead to many performance problems.

Afterwards, the developers learn how to create procedural objects like functions and procedures, and they see how a stored procedure is similar to a void function. The programmers learn all these things; they can use their familiar programming language and they are very happy!

DATABASE LOYALTY IS LOYALTY MISPLACED

I have met people who are devoted to specific database systems. These people consider themselves programmers for that specific database only. For example, Joe is a PL/SQL developer while Joanna is a Transact-SQL developer. Neither would ever move to another database system under any circumstances! This is a bad decision, in my opinion. Let's see why.

The programming languages just mentioned are actually a **mixture**. PL SQL, for example, is a language composed of two types of instructions: **SQL** statements and **procedural** statements. All of these programming languages are a kind of query-programming languages due to their mixed nature. In the database, in a stored procedure or a function, you are always in the position to execute either a SQL statement or a procedural statement. Whenever you want to query something, mostly to read or write data, you use SQL. The database programming language is an extension of the query language; it's not like a classic programming language. This is a big difference! The programmer needs to be capable of querying the data: this is his first task. Anything else is secondary.

The Advantage of a Standard

Another advantage of SQL is the fact that it is a **standard**. This means that the set of instructions is available in a very similar or even identical manner from one programming language to another. Every database programming language uses SQL in its own way. Still, most of the syntaxes are very close to the standard. For example, a select statement (a query) is almost the same in Oracle and SQL Server and in other relational databases systems. This also applies to update and insert statements. There are variations and differences but it's very easy to move and write from one programming language to another. You don't need to feel uncomfortable when switching.

Portability should not be a goal in itself. If I had to choose between **portability** and **performance**, I would always choose performance. Sometimes performance means writing SQL according to the specific syntax and not necessarily according to the standard. For example, in SQL Server, the updates are particular and they cannot be migrated to Oracle or others database systems even if it is pure SQL. However, it is not very difficult to translate one SQL to another if the performance is better. If there is a similar performance, portability is desired. Anyway, the existence of a standard assures maximum portability by itself.

To conclude, do we have something like database programming? The answer is definitely yes. However, the programming language means maybe 80% query language and maybe 20% of the extension. A good database developer is a very good SQL developer, or so they should be. The programming languages, the extensions, were made so that developers could certain things that couldn't be accomplished using basic SQL. The set of procedural statements should be used when the problems cannot be solved with a simple SQL statement. Database programming mostly means SQL development, because data access is our goal when we are in the database. In addition, data access is SQL!

Programming Is a Practical Activity

Software development is a highly practical occupation. Most programmers are practical people, not scientists. The most difficult part of their job is the struggle with one business or another, trying to understand it.

IT universities should be aware of these realities. From what I know, there are serious differences between education systems. Without judging any of these systems, I can objectively say some words about some tendencies. In some places, the programming courses are highly theoretical and thus too far away from the practical reality of software development. Math is the foundation but this does not mean students need to go deeper than necessary. I have been doing database programming for many years and the math that I use is high school level.

Math is a world in itself. It is almost a perfect world and certainly a very beautiful world. Programming is our practical world: our economy, our education, our sports, our industry, our hobbies, everything.

A programmer needs to be able to understand different businesses and to adapt his knowledge to them. He should be one of us, not a savant far away from our world. The programmers need to be able to understand different businesses and to adapt their knowledge to them. They should be one of us, not some sort of savants far away from our world.

If you want to build an application for a game, you need to understand that game, you need to understand the rules that the game needs to follow, and you need to play the game.

Programming is not science, programming is not math, and programming is not differential equations! Programming is life, programming means the ability to live in our world, and the ability to understand and implement one business or another. This is actually the main reason why programmers are valuable people. The engineer learns and implements all kinds of technologies technology, the doctor learns to cure and heal others, and the taxi driver knows the roads like no one else. The programmer needs to be able to understand each of these businesses and more, also needs to be aware of how to implement any given business into a software application.

A programming language is not a difficult thing by itself. It is true that not anyone can understand and write programs in a certain programming language; certain skills are required. You need to have a logical mind; you must understand what an algorithm is and how to implement it in a language. You need to have a solid math background, but it is not necessary to be a mathematician. These skills are not as rare as many people might think. Moreover, there is no reason to say that programming is a man's occupation. Ladies have the same skills as men and it is rather frustrating that such a small number of women participate,comparing to that of men.

A large numbers of teenagers avoid moving into this area due to lack of self-confidence. I have some good news for these people: programming is much easier than you think. Just try it!

What is difficult in programming it is not the language itself and not the set of theoretical knowledge that you learn in universities. The difficulty consists in the ability to understand what is to be implemented, in the ability to live and model the life. Because the businesses that are modelled by our applications are part of our society; they are parts of our life. What is more complex in this world than us?

Is Database Programming Special?

Now, let's move back to our goal: database development. The students, the young programmers, the application developers with little background in database development, all of these user groups should be able to understand and deal with data.

Data is everywhere, and programmers deal with it all the time. In most cases, the data is relational. Despite appearances, the data requires a certain type of understanding and, for that, a different kind of effort is required. Database development is that kind of programming that deals with data in a relational format, which means rows and columns. We need it, whether we like it or not, and we need to see if our styles are appropriate for this purpose. When I say "our styles," I am referring to the classic styles that we are familiar with from the user interface level.

Most programmers follow the model of general programming that they learned in college. However, the relational model and the database are different and particular and, in many cases, a different style is required.

For example, let's examine the reality of a factory. This reality consists of a sum of processes that are handled in the factory, the multitude of documents that are used in the factory, and the different sets of calculations that are done in the production business inside the factory. We want to build a software application to reflect the reality of this enterprise. For that, we may use different models.

No matter the model, relevant business data needs to be stored in a dedicated space called the database. This business data can consist of a list of materials, with the multitude of material attributes, like the type of products, different classifications, the list of components or bills for materials for the finished products, the list of accountancy documents, company documents, and others. Some of these documents may be generated from others. Considering this example of production, it is clear that the segment of data storage is one of the most critical, maybe the most important one.

There is the user interface and the database. The developers spend time in both places. They can do their work in the same manner in both sections, at the user interface and at the database level. Alternatively, they can do the work differently when they are involved in the database layer and they can use a distinct style in concordance with the nature of data. Both approaches are considered database programming, but I believe that the second approach is fundamentally better.

I think that we should write in the database in a certain way. Moreover, the way we should write couldn't be derived directly from the style we use at the user interface level and from the two classic models. The fact that this database way is particular and is derived from the nature of data does not make any difference and is not a counter argument. The main reason for this book is to illustrate this way and to promote it.

The SQL Shop Metaphor

I hope you will excuse the apparent deviation from the neutral style of this book. I invite you to step into a world of metaphors and analogies. Imagine you fell asleep and you found yourself transported into a fantasy shop. This is the **SQL Shop**.

Welcome to my shop! While shopping, I hope to demonstrate two dominant keywords: **simplicity** and **naturalness**.

My shop is a chocolate shop. There are so many types of chocolate from different countries. Please feel free to take a look. Read the names of the different types of chocolate. Terrifc; you have **selected** different brands to read more about them. Oh, even better; you have **inserted** them into your shopping cart.

Did you notice the use of the most important keywords in SQL: **select** and **insert**. First, you need to have the possibility of select information before choosing something to buy. You read the instructions on different products in the shop and you looked at the design of the products. You analyzed the utility of each product, and you decided which product fit your taste and budget. This is the select operation, or the read phase. No one is able to write without being able to read first.

Next, you decided what to buy. You chose the selected products and inserted them into your basket. The basket is filled with the **inserted** products. This **inserted** keyword sounds familiar to some SQL Server developers. Is it similar to a temporary table attached to any insert trigger? Isn't it fascinating that we can talk about a simple situation like buying candy and we can easily segue into discussing SQL? This is just one example of why SQL is so valuable: due to the naturalness of the language. SQL is really a part of our life!

The database is like a shop. You can think of the data in a database as a list of goods in a supermarket, or a list of books in a library. Whenever you enter a market or a shop, you can read and understand the utility of the products, comparing benefits and disadvantages. This is the select phase. This is the read section.

You can also fill your cart with some products. This is the insert phase. You insert some chosen products into the basket. You can also choose, after reflecting and analyzing your budget, to dismiss some products before you pay; in other words, you **delete** them from your list of products. This delete keyword seems very familiar, doesn't it? You can also decide to replace an object with another similar object, requiring an **update** to your shopping list.

Everything can change until the moment you arrive at the counter to pay. This period of indecision can take some time, maybe even a day or two. What if you are called away from the counter by an emergency right before you commit the transaction? The store staff would have to **rollback** the items in the cart, restocking the shelves with your unpurchased products.

Does this language sound technical? I don't think so, do you? This is the beauty of SQL!

This shop is the database. The items are the rows in different tables, the tables may be considered as the brands. The shopping period is a database transaction. During this period, you have the freedom to add, remove, or change items in the basket. Like in the database, you have the option to select, update, insert, or delete the rows. After the payment, changes are not permitted to the basket, unless a new shopping session starts. The transaction commit is the payment.

This analogy between a shop and a database, between the list of items in a basket and the list of affected rows in a transaction, between the payment and the transaction commit, shows the simplicity of the database model and the naturalness of SQL. You will see more examples throughout this book.

An Example of Bad Practice

Now let's consider a programming example. I was once on a contract where I needed to build a data migration system between two sources of data. There was an existing system and I was required to build a new data migration interface. I analyzed this migration system and I tried to understand what was going on in it.

For example, there was a very simple step inside this migration system: some configuration values were required in a certain table. One table was the target for this step, and three or four columns needed to be updated with highly static values. This table was configured once and these configuration values were to be used all over the place in the corresponding application. These values were not to be changed afterwards. Let me explain how this step was built. A stored procedure was written for this purpose; this was normal because the configuration values were critical values so the step was very distinct. Nevertheless, looking at the stored procedure, I was forced to spend some time to understand the goal of this step.

What I found was unbelievable. Some structures were declared and used, with some types; one cursor was used; and everything was so complicated! When I realized that the actual goal of this step was simply to add three or four values in a table and add one row with some configuration data, I started to laugh! I said to myself that this is not possible. The programmer that wrote that code, a specific bit of PL/SQL code, was coming from the user interface and completely ignores the fact that the environment of work was a relational database! The same style and the same patterns as in Java or C++ or whatever application language were used! I was amazed!

Once I realized that the goal of this particular step was actually to add one line in a table, I simply rewrote the procedure completely and added an insert statement. The entire data migration interface was written in this style, many structures and types, with cursors over cursors!

This data migration system is a very good example of what happens if a row-by-row approach and a pure procedural style are used in a data migration application. The PL SQL language was used like a typical and classic language. That programmer tried to develop in a pure object-oriented style.

It was a disaster! First, the performance was at the **minimum** level. That software application had a very poor performance, and the indexes and performance features were useless due to the **inappropriate style of programming**. When I rebuilt the data migration interface, everything was rewritten in pure SQL. I had maybe one or two cursors in the entire data migration interface. There were no structures, no arrays and no cursors: just pure SQL! After that, the performance of the new data migration utility was at the **maximum** level. Even better, the data migration system was very simple for anyone to understand. It made a huge difference!

Many data-oriented software applications are not correctly written. The performance is the first thing that suffers, and the code is more complicated than it should be. When you are in the database and when your task is to manipulate data, you need to think SQL; you need to think in **data sets**. You need to try to understand the relational model and appreciate the clarity of this model and the naturalness of SQL.

The database programming languages are just extensions of SQL. PL/SQL is a programming language but is an extension for SQL. A good database programmer knows that SQL is the first priority and the extension (the set of procedural statements) is more like a backup solution for SQL. The philosophy is simple: You have a problem, so try to solve it in SQL. If this is not possible, go to the extension and use the set of procedural statements. Why use a cursor when you can solve your problem with a simple SQL statement?

Let's end this chapter with another shop analogy. Imagine that you want to buy 20 bottles of wine and 30 bottles of water. Try to imagine, for a moment, that you will fill the basket 30 times for the wine and 20 times for the water. You will pay 50 times in total. How long would that take? Far too long. A normal person will fill the basket once and will pay for the set of 20 bottles of wine and the second set of 30 bottles of water. Any reasonable person will try to fill just one basket; eventuall will try to limit it to two baskets. Anyway, the latter approach will save a good deal of time.

Now imagine that you have an update statement and you will affect 20 products in the update instruction. Many programmers would consider it normal to process the rows one by one. Instead of thinking of this as a set of rows and trying to affect that set of rows via a simple SQL statement, they start declaring structures, variables, and eventually try to use complex objects only because they can't or don't want to think SQL!

CHAPTER 3

■ ■ ■

A Holistic Vision of the Data

I will continue with the theoretical discussions about the two styles of development and I will introduce you to the key concept behind one of the styles of development. This is the concept that identifies one style against the other: the concept of the data set. I will explain that the concept of style, despite its degree of subjectivity, is a notion that should be analyzed by a variety of professionals in a variety of environments, starting with IT universities and continuing with software companies.

I will explain how people need to think when following one approach or another, by opposition, and to show the advantages of one approach over another. I will describe some alternates paths to database development and delimit the set-based approach somehow in the general picture.

I will explain that the role of the data set in the development activity in a relational database is crucial for good performance in that database.

The Concept of the Data Set

The concept of a data set is related to the SQL language, which is mainly a query language. The purpose of the language is straightforward: data access. Data in a relational database means a mixture of rows and columns or expressions. In most cases, when accessing data you are identifying a **combination of rows and columns or expressions**, and this is the description of a **data set**.

The one constant when dealing with data and database programming is a set of data. There is always a data set; there is always a combination of rows and columns or expressions whenever you are dealing with data. All the mysteries and solutions of database development rely on the proper treatment and fair recognition of the data set.

The Importance of the Data Set

Data sets can be taken from a variety of tables linked by joins. Data sets can be combined by set operators, and data sets can be identified in a variety of ways that are not relevant for the moment. The SQL developer is the magician who knows how to get the best from the data set.

If there is one thing that defines the development process in a database (like the class or an entity in object-oriented programming) it is the data set. Of course there are

© Stefan Ardeleanu 2016
S. Ardeleanu, *Relational Database Programming*, DOI 10.1007/978-1-4842-2080-1_3

other concepts and terms. I was once working with a team of Java developers on a project. They were discussing entities and I was discussing tables! These are various perspectives on the same thing, in one way or another. So, someone else might say that the table is the main keyword to define databases.

Comparing the two, you can see that the table precedes the data set, because the data set itself extracts everything from the table. My opinion is that, from the development process, the data set is more granular. Whenever you have a relational database, you have the table with rows and columns. This is a reality. You can develop in any way and handle the data in the table in many ways. One of these paths is the set-based one. In choosing this development approach, you choose the data set as the key to your development process.

SQL and the Data Set

Most of the practices that follow illustrate this major characteristic of database programming and SQL. Database programming means firstly SQL development, and SQL is the bread and the butter of any vendor programming language, be it PL/SQL or another variety.

The main activity in the database is the process of querying. You are querying the data continuously because this is the essence of database programming. You always try to get a combination of rows and columns or expressions taken from various tables; you always try to get a set of data. This is the secret of SQL, and more than that, this is the secret of database programming: try to think in **sets** of data and do not think atomically, whenever possible.

▪ **Tip**   Do not try to divide a data set into smaller units unless you have an authentic business reason to do so or a technical limitation that stops you from affecting the data set as a whole.

Try to have the following vision of data: see the data as an integer and not as a sum of decimals. If the data set corresponds to one row, this is a particular situation. Always try to find the set of data; try to think in waves of data, like waves in the ocean. When you see a wave coming from the sea, you never imagine any division; you just see the wave and admire it! Looking closely you can divide the wave into smaller sections according to various classifications. However, initially you don't care about that! Try this with the data set and you will think like a true database developer!

A Mix of Art and Science

I am not a theoretician but I admire theoreticians. They have great minds and they are capable of things beyond ordinary people like me. Theoreticians can build foundations. These foundations are the base for human creations everywhere. Software programming is a new world in terms of history. It is a child, a growing one!

Every programming language is a miracle, in one way or another. Programmers who have the ability to write pieces of software are like artists and linguists in a certain way; they're not just pure technicians.

Every new programming language that we learn to use is like a new natural language that we learn to speak. Some languages are easier to learn than others. In a similar fashion, some programming languages are easier to teach than others. It is a matter of subjectivity and experience, as well as a matter of taste. Some languages and frameworks can be learned by analogy and comparison.

SQL and Portability

Speaking about the set of database programming languages, like PL/SQL or Transact SQL, there is another great advantage, one of portability. SQL is part of every relational database programming language and, even if there are some differences in the syntaxes, learning one means learning another is quite easy. I am referring, of course, to the list of programming languages associated to the relational database systems like Oracle, SQL Server, DB2, My SQL, Teradata, etc.

The procedural facilities are also similar. The syntax of declaring and using a cursor in Oracle and SQL Server and DB2 is very similar. You don't need to consider yourself only a PL/SQL developer and remain in the area of PL/SQL.

Operating on Data Sets

Let's assume that you are running a query. You just saw the familiar message about the number of rows affected; let's say you receive five rows. The affected five rows may be interpreted in many ways. You may think in terms of five details, try to analyze the details, and think of the details in a certain way. Alternatively, you can think about the five rows as one unit. It is this latter way of thinking that leads you to the data set.

The set of five rows can be seen as a whole or it can be seen as a sum of details. The application developer is tempted to see the multiplicity and is tempted to divide the set into five pieces. He might open a cursor right away. By contrast, the database developer will always see the data set; he will be aware of it and he will think SQL. This means he will try to see the data set and ignore the fact that the data set can be divided into five pieces. The application developer is not SQL oriented by default; he is oriented to search for the details. His models are not set-oriented and he is trying, by default, to divide and to use the procedural features of the language.

Two Approaches

SQL is data set-oriented, SQL is a database-specific language, and SQL is not incorporated in the paradigm of the classic models of programming. The application developers should make an effort to try to integrate SQL into their style; they should try to be aware of the data set. The application developers should do these things if they want to have good performance in the database and especially if their intended goal is to transfer data between systems. They should be able to adapt.

Considering these circumstances, I will define two approaches that can be used in database programming. These are illustrated by the role of the set of data in the process of database development. These approaches are the ones that map the development styles, and the developers should use a certain style according to the approaches they follow.

The first is the **atomic** approach. By contrast, I will name its opposite the **holistic** approach. These are the possible visions of the data in database programming. Consequently, the styles of development will be highly influenced by these.

The programmer that follows the atomic vision is the programmer who thinks atomically, the programmer who does not think SQL. The atomic vision means to divide everything and to see things at the **row** level. The developers do not accept anything apart from what they know; they know structured programming, they know scalar functions and row triggers, and they see columns per individual rows as parameters for their functions and procedures. They believe that the purpose of a cursor is to allow them to move everything at the level of a row. The atomic vision does not consider the data set at all.

The holistic approach is the opposite approach. These programmers are aware of another kind of entity apart from what they know from classic programming: they knows that SQL is something else and they understand that the data set is an integer, and they think holistically.

They have the data set and they want to affect that set with any possible means. They use SQL as the tool to accomplish that. As a last resource, if SQL does not allow them to perform their tasks and to affect the data set holistically, they will divide everything using the cursor and they will solve his problem in a different way.

Data Sets as Atomic Units

I will prove that a set of data should be analyzed in its atomicity, not its multiplicity. In most situations, the data set can be identified as such and affected as a unit. The data set should be targeted and, finally, affected by our actions, write or read. When working in the database, in a classic but mostly in a specific application, we affect data sets in a continuous process. We should be aware of the data set; we should always think of it and try not to divide it into smaller pieces or rows whenever possible.

Let's remember the famous concept of an entity, so dear to application developers. In classic programming, everything is an entity or part of an entity. The entity is a very complex concept, and programmers are always aware of the belongings of a certain entity when they are doing their work. In the database, we can say that the role of the entity is taken by the data set. The data set is the entity, and in a relational database we are usually positioned in a certain data set.

Like a Chameleon

Operating on data sets as units is the holistic approach, and the developer that thinks holistically is a true SQL developer, a true database developer. In addition, this is the kind of transformation that an application developer should be capable of when switching to the database. I believe that a good programmer can do things at a good level in both the application and database. Consequently, I believe that programmers should think differently and adapt their style when moving to the database.

Another purpose of this book is to get you to think SQL! Because the dedicated language for communicating with the data is SQL, its syntax is perfect for interrogating rows and columns. Most situations in a database are simply accessing the data in one way or another.

When I want to read or write something, I use SQL. That's why I am always surprised when I hear database developers consider themselves PL/SQL developers or P-SQL developers. To me, a true database developer is a SQL developer. Moreover, a SQL developer, a good one, needs to be able to think SQL. Thinking SQL means thinking in sets of data. I cannot imagine anyone thinking PL/SQL or Transact SQL!

Thinking in Data Sets

Let's continue looking at the advantages of the SQL language. The actions in the database are restricted to basic statements. Let's review them. We read some data using a **SELECT** statement, we add something using an **INSERT** statement, we edit something using an **UPDATE** statement, or we delete something using a **DELETE** statement. This is what database programming is. In almost all situations, we want to affect a set of rows, one single set. A good SQL developer is always aware of the data set: he tries to search for the data set. This is the holistic vision: this means thinking SQL and this is true database development! Only in the rare situations when the data set cannot be handled as a **whole** will the programmer split the data set into its **details** and eventually use the procedural facilities.

The database programmers are not the limited programmers who do not accept anything but the data set and their precious SQL! These guys are not absurd! The database developers know the principles of structured programming: they know how to use cursors, records, variables, while statements, and the rest of the procedural features. They can solve the problem even if the data set vision does not match all the time. The data set is not indestructible! It can always be divided! Sometimes the data set must be divided into many pieces. The holistic vision accepts the possibility of the division whenever it's necessary.

The atomic path means the tendency to divide things right away and to solve things procedurally by default. No attempt is made generally for the data set to be handled; the data set is not actually seen as a unit. The atomic vision is very common among many application developers and I point is that this vision should be reconsidered.

A **holistic** vision of the data will generate a certain distinct style of development in the database. First, you identify the data set. Next, you analyze the data and see if it can be affected by one single SQL statement. If that is possible, and very often it is because SQL is incredible strong and it covers an amazing number of situations, the problem can be solved at the level of the entire set. This is the holistic vision and the set prioritization. This is the **set-oriented model of database development**.

Take Style Seriously

The education systems are an important component of the IT industry. The universities teach the students about classes, entities, objects, and everything else. The object-oriented models, the declarative programming, and the structured programming paradigms are described in a variety of courses. There are many models and paradigms, and each of them should be taught to the future generations of programmers. These principles and models will guide the future programmers in their activity and will influence their work and our lives.

Let's move back to the database area. Most people think that database programming is part of structured programming. Apart from typical programming and the classic models, there are courses about databases where relational databases are explained. The SQL language is at the top of the list. Sometimes SQL is explained by itself in a dedicated course or it is described as part of a vendor programming language like PL/SQL. Programing languages such as PL/SQL can be described in two steps: first the query language and then the extension with all the procedural facilities.

I believe that there is not enough discussion about the styles of programming, and this is understandable. The concept of style is a vague concept and it involves a certain degree of subjectivity. However, no one can argue that these various styles of development are not important and that our applications are not influenced by this vague concept of style. It is only because style is a subjective matter that it is ignored.

The style of development is influenced by the subjectivity of the programmer too. Some programmers are Java-based and they are comfortable with Java; others like INFORMATICA and visual development and they are comfortable with it. And the subjectivity of the programmer is influenced by the concepts in the language being used. It's a vicious circle.

Understanding the Data Set

In teaching programming, I believe that the concept of the **data set** should be properly described as one of the main concepts in database programming, maybe the most important one. I think that the paradigm of **set-oriented programming** should be promoted in database courses in universities and explained as a priority to the students. Many programmers will work on both sides during their careers. They will work at the application level using Java or C# but they will also work at the database level using Oracle or DB2. If they know about the data set and the holistic approach, it will be easier for them to adapt to one style to another. For those who want to specialize in database development, understanding of the importance of the data set is critical.

The Importance of Style

For example, let's pick a university where database programming is supported and is considered a valuable path for students. In this university, the database programming courses should contain a second part, after the classic SQL course, where the capabilities of SQL are explained. This second part should discuss database development and the importance of the data set and the holistic vision of development. It should explain that a different style should be used in the database, one based on the set-based approach and a holistic vision of data.

I also believe that discussions on style are very important inside software development teams. Teams often consist of application and database developers. Moreover, there are always personal preferences. The software applications are influenced by these preferences.

I believe that performance will be better if a more appropriate style is used. It will increase the quality of the written software. Although the users can't see the database, they can feel it all the time because of the response timings.

Programming as a Distinct Path

Let's move to the specialized database developers and their role in the market. I believe that the role of database developers will increase. I believe that the concept of database developer finally has its own status, without being in the shadow of Java or C. There are more and more specialized database developers, and the good ones are always aware of the data set and of the set-oriented style of development that they definitely use!

Still, many people believe that database programming is not necessarily a distinct path and that it does not require a distinct style. Many people believe that an application developer can do SQL easily without needing to change anything in the style of work. There are no official arguments for a different style, and there are so many programmers doing both application and database programming.

In a classic system, things may be acceptable with a procedural, atomic style. However, in a **specific** interface like a replication system or an ETL where the goal is to move data between systems, if the developers are working atomically it's a tragedy; it's the most catastrophic scenario that we can imagine!

Unfortunately, SQL is sometimes seen as a kind of toy, as a light language that can be learned by anyone with a minimal effort. To a certain degree, it is a toy, and it is true that the basics can be accomplished by anyone; the language is extremely natural and intuitive. That is merely the first stage of learning. Imagine a class that is separated into many modules, and the first module is very easy and accessible. The following modules are more and more difficult. This is SQL.

Promoting the Holistic Style

From this perspective, the concept of a **data set** makes a difference in graduating to the next module. A programmer that understands this concept and follows it is a good database developer. For example, Joanna Doe is an application developer who is switching from the application to the database. If she can change her style and adapt her work from one section to another, she will be able to accomplish a lot. I really believe that the set-based approach and the holistic style of development deserve to be promoted more intensively, considering the advantages of better performance, easier debugging, and more intelligible code.

Let's consider one more example. Think of a list of customers that satisfy certain conditions, such as customers from London, UK. If you are thinking SQL, you will think of them as a set of customers. This is the SQL vision! You don't consider the customers in their multiplicity; you think of the list of customer as one list. This vision is opposed to the atomic vision, where you would think of the customers as single units. This is what I consider the principle of SQL. We consider multiplicity as unity. As another example, if you have a book that's 100 pages long, you think of it as one book, not 100 pages.

Inside projects, the project managers have an important role. Taking various styles of development in various sections into consideration is important if they want good performance and good code.

A large portion of our code relies on the databases: the vendors continuously try to add new features for the performance section. Performance is always critical. What can be more unpleasant than waiting and waiting for the data to be accessible to the end users? One reason for a bad performance in the database is the fact that the style of development is not adapted to the realities of the databases.

The Benefits

I know that most programmers are very practical people and they want to see written code as proof of concepts. To that end, I will illustrate the concepts described above and the two alternative programming styles by showing many examples. I will use two of the most important database systems, Oracle and Microsoft SQL Server. I chose these two database management systems for my examples for two simple reasons. First, they are among the most popular database management systems. Secondly, I personally have a lot of experience with these two systems. I have experience in classic applications and in specific applications like data warehouse, replication, and data migration. These are my favorite types of projects and during them I was able to adapt my style more and more to the **set-oriented approach**.

Nevertheless, these examples are very easy to reproduce in any other database management system. This is another advantage of the standard—the fact that most SQL statements are identical or similar in almost all relational database systems. This advantage will allow any developer who wants to try the exercises in Oracle, SQL Server, DB2, PostgreSQL, MySQL, and Teradata to do so. The programmer can practice most of the exercises with minor modifications.

This is another argument in the favor of the holistic approach, although I do not consider it the most important one. The argument is **portability**. This is good for companies building software applications for various database management systems for different customers: portability is an attractive word for managers. If you are at a software company where one application is written in several systems like Oracle, SQL Server, and My SQL, portability is important. Writing SQL allows you to keep the code similar from one system to another. In contrast, working procedurally means accepting very different pieces of codes because, even if the procedural languages are quite similar, there are still different syntaxes and it takes some time to translate the code from one system to another.

The examples in the atomic approach are taken from the procedural area of the systems. These are highly particular and non-standard, being non-SQL and procedural. Working atomically forces you to move your center of interest in the procedural area of the database language. In the atomic way, the logic is procedural and specific to the programming language, which materializes in a serious effort in the translation process, if required. When I say procedural I am mostly refer to Oracle relational database system. However, even if Transact SQL is declared itself as a declarative language comparing with PL SQL that is considered a procedural language, a lot of tasks can be achieved non-SQL in both SQL Server and Oracle.

Working in SQL moves you to the SQL area, close to the standard and to the true database vision. If you try to reproduce some examples from one system to another, it's much easier. It may even be very easy because often the logic and syntax is identical.

Be Independent

I am discussing SQL. I am trying to show you how to think SQL. This makes you more independent in the database system. In addition, if you are working in an IT company that creates software, it is very easy for you to maintain various logic in different systems if your work is SQL based and not procedurally based.

Many database programmers have exclusive experience in one database system. Some of them believe they are Oracle or PL/SQL developers. Having SQL as a standard makes our lives easier, and I encourage any developer of this type to consider himself a neutral database developer, or even better, a SQL developer.

Even with procedural facilities, things are not very difficult. Most of the examples can be easily migrated and executed in any relational database system. They offer the same types of programming objects and similar structures of blocks inside the objects; cursors are declared and used in similar ways. In the field of programming, the database developers have a huge advantage. For a database programmer, one experience in any database system is a gate to any other database system, and the database programmers need to have more confidence in themselves regarding their ability. For example, many experienced SQL Server programmers are not confident in switching to Oracle projects. Of course, an initial effort is required to understand the differences but this is not that difficult.

The switch is especially straightforward if the style of the programmer is SQL-oriented and not procedural oriented. A lot of code is pretty much the same. Writing mainly SQL and being in concordance with the standard allows us to write very similarly in different database systems and this is a great advantage!

Even if we do write SQL, there are many ways of writing SQL. There are various SQL syntaxes, and some can be more standard and others more specific. Sometimes a specific SQL syntax offers better performance. A good example is the SQL Server particular form of update. This syntax has a better performance and, despite the fact that is particular to SQL Server, it's the one to use. When a compromise between performance and portability is required, I always vote for performance.

I want to conclude the discussions about portability and performance in database development and share my opinions gathered from years of experience with various databases. The first rule, to write SQL and not procedural, is a golden rule for both performance and portability. The second conclusion refers to the SQL code itself. The code is similar, sometimes identical in various database systems. When the code is similar, there are many acceptable syntaxes. Sometimes you may use the specific syntaxes and avoid the identical ones because very often the specific syntaxes have better performance. A good example is the specific form of update and delete in SQL Server; although this doesn't work in Oracle, I encourage you to use it and leave the syntax with subqueries because the performance for the specific DML is better. Again, choose performance over portability.

Visual vs. SQL Development

There is a new generation of programmers. I call them visual developers. This new category of programmers is becoming more and more appreciated on the market. To remain in the field of databases, let's consider data warehousing. I am especially thinking of the ETL process of extracting, transforming, and loading the data from a set of operational systems to a large data warehouse system, a historical database. There are many examples of ETL visual tools, like INFORMATICA, Oracle Warehouse Builder, or Microsoft Integration Services.

An ETL process is a very complicated process where data needs to be integrated from various operational systems into a historical database, with the purpose of analysis and prediction. An ETL developer nowadays is sometimes a visual developer and not a classic developer. Of course the best ones are both because even a visual developer will need to debug and know the sources behind the visual tool. Therefore, especially when speaking about specific interfaces like a replication system, an ETL, or a data migration system, whenever we are discussing the transfer of data between systems, a visual tool might be a solution. Managers very often choose these types of solutions.

We are slowly moving to a mixed world. The future world will also be the world of tools: this seems to be the tendency. Consequently, the future world will be a world of visual developers, too. To be a good specialist today does not necessarily mean to be a good classic programmer of a certain type, like a C# programmer. You can be a very good visual programmer.

Choosing a Tool or a Language

I have some experience in visual development but I do not intend to move to this area. I like SQL too much. Moreover, in my experience, choosing a tool instead of a custom solution with SQL is not a good decision. I affirm that with the SQL language, you can do miracles and very often the use of tools can be avoided and replaced with pure SQL systems. I don't believe you can build a better replication system or data migration system with a tool than with pure SQL. Of course, visual developers will disagree and it is their right to do so; I am sure they have solid arguments too. Not being a visual developer, I respect their arguments and their options. However, my experience with visual tools showed me that the argument of time is not necessary valid. I am not certain that the development time with a visual tool is indeed better than the development time with a classic, non-visual approach. Moreover, sometimes when you have problems in a visual tool, it is almost impossible to move forward!

It is clear that there are various alternatives on the market and this is great. Companies can choose. There is more and more demand for the **specific** type of software application, with the clear goal of data movement between existing systems. Companies are moving their data continuously; there is a huge demand for this task almost everywhere, and companies try to find better solutions to satisfy their goals. Sometimes they are not satisfied with true database specialists and classic database development and they prefer to move to tools and visual development instead.

I am on the SQL side! I think that often a task can be achieved with simple and pure database programming, with simple SQL and using ordinary database development tools like Oracle SQL Developer or Microsoft SQL Server Management Studio, even in the ETL area, which is maybe the most complex case of pure database system. I once built a very complex replication and data migration system (similar to an ETL system) and I did it in pure SQL, using something like 5% procedural code. In addition, it works great, I know what is there and I understand everything, and I have the perspective of the whole and of the details. Developers who come after me can understand all of the migration steps.

This task, of moving data between different systems, can be done in most cases with pure SQL. For that, we need to have the proper developers to do that.

I can say, based on my experience as a contractor, tools represent a bit of danger. A person working in a certain tool for five years may become completely dependent on that tool. The second problem is the fact that most of these tools are visual. For example, in the ETL area, almost everything is done within the complex visual diagrams. Many people are not aware of anything apart from their diagrams. I feel that many of these tool specialists have a limited understanding of the whole picture.

Use SQL

Anyway, using a custom solution with authentic database programmers is possible and if the complexity allows, it gives the company the advantage of not being dependent on the tool and the tool specialists. It also provides the company with the possibility of a product and to understand its own work. In many cases, the solutions with the tools are more expensive and less efficient than the traditional solution that use SQL and database programmers.

Speaking of tools, the fact that visual development is easier than classic development is an illusion. The reason for visual tools is speed and efficiency. Things can be done faster and more efficiently with visual tools. The visual developer works fast compared to the classic developer. At first, this seems true. Allow me to express my doubts and to affirm that, in many cases, using a pure SQL solution for a specific interface can be faster, with a better performance, better control, and more understanding of the system.

CHAPTER 4

■ ■ ■

Data by Set or by Row?

This book is divided in two parts. The first part describes the concepts and the second part illustrates these concepts with practical examples. With these examples I want to show that, very often, the same task within a database can be done either using the **atomic** style of programming, a common style used by many application developers, or using the **holistic** approach for data access, the true SQL style of programming, a style that is specific to authentic database programmers. You will see that this latter style of programming is much simpler and more accurate. The code is much simpler, the performance is better, and the code is highly portable from one database system to another. Actually, I don't see any advantage of the atomic approach over the holistic approach (of course, these considerations apply to the specific context of database development).

When I refer to true database developers and an authentic database development approach, I don't mean to say that a set-based style is an exclusive style that should be used exclusively by specialized database developers. This style is different and, with some effort, it can be accommodated by application developers working in a database relatively easy. They don't need to change their style completely; they can obviously continue to write in the same manner at the application level. But when moving from the user interface to the database they should adjust their style to think holistically and write SQL, as much as they can.

Database developers think in sets almost natively because they are a kind of mercenaries of the **set-based approach**; they do not follow the atomic approach unless it's required. They find the atomic approach as totally inadequate, inefficient, and counterintuitive. For database developers, the set-oriented approach is the obvious way of doing things. This approach is not so clear to the application developers, so they need to spend some time to understand and accommodate this new approach. However, this is not a very difficult task and, as soon as they understand it, it's infinitely more efficient in the database. All these considerations apply to **classic** applications, where both approaches are acceptable in the database.

■ **Note**   I want to mention again the specific data migration applications, where the **goal is to move data between various database systems**. In these **specific** software systems, the atomic approach is completely forbidden and the application developers should stay away from these applications if they do not want to change the way they write code!

Choosing the Level of Detail

One of the main tasks for anyone working in a database is querying and returning the required information. This is why a query language like SQL was invented: this language is dedicated to this purpose. SQL is a natural language and its naturalness is derived from the limited purpose of the language. You can never compare SQL to a classic programming language! A query language like SQL is highly particular and applies to the data organized in a relational manner. This is why, basically, it is easy to learn SQL.

SQL is never on its own. The set of SQL instructions is always embedded in a programming language. I am using PL/SQL for Oracle or Transact SQL for SQL Server in this book. There are many relational database systems and associated languages, and Oracle and SQL Server are just the examples that I prefer to use.

All of these programming languages contain two types of instructions: SQL statements and procedural, eventually declarative, statements. There is an alternative for any programmer. Your logic can rely more on SQL statements or it can rely more on procedural statements. You can think more procedurally or you can think more SQL. In most of the cases, the procedural way is associated with the atomic approach. However, it is possible to work holistically and procedurally, as you will see in some examples later in the book.

There are many levels of details in our logic when we write code in the database. There is always the **lowest** level of detail, the **row** itself. In most cases, a **superior** level of detail should be present, the **data set** to be affected. Very often, the data is identified and updated in data sets. In most cases, we are in a position to choose what level to pick up. The traditional models don't know about the data set because this concept is particular to relational databases. Consequently, the application developers coming from Java or C, and their traditional models, should become familiar with the data set; otherwise they will be tempted to remain at the lowest level of detail, the **data row**.

Working Atomically

The application developers will start opening cursors for every action, declaring variables, and using records to supply simple insert statements. By contrast, the database developers are able to think SQL. The database developers know that they need to identify the **data set** and will rely on SQL statements instead of procedural statements to make the identification because they will choose the level of detail at the data set and not the data row. The database developers know that the SQL language is a **set-oriented language** and know that this is what should be used in most of their development activity.

For any programmer working in the database and trying to manage the data either by reading something or by writing information, a decision must be made regarding how to write the logic. What is the starting point? What is the concept that stays behind the scene in this strange and simple world of rows and columns? The application developers, used to objects and entities, need now to understand the simpler concept of rows and columns and the concept of the data set. Very often, they see that the procedural facilities available in the dedicated programming languages for data access are applicable to the lowest level of detail. For example, they think the scalar function, a row trigger, and even loop and while statements are excellent for data access at the lowest level of detail: the row itself.

Consequently, the application developers believe that they always need to move the logic to the lowest level of detail, the row. They believe it's normal for code to be written and applicable to the lowest level of detail. This is a bad decision in my opinion and it leads to poor performance in many databases. Writing data access logic in this manner, when the principle is to move the logic by default to the lowest level of detail and to use the atomic style, is the worst programming someone can write in the database!

Do you know what's funny? The resulting row-level code may look very professional and attractive to classic programmers. All the principles of structured programming are satisfied, and this code may look like a piece of art. This shows once more the subjectivity of the concept of style of programming!

Row-by-Row Performance

The atomic approach is not wrong and it will generate the desired results. However, the effects of row-by-row processing are dramatic and the consequences are terrible for the database. First, the performance is a disaster. Imagine large data sets affected by cursors all the time, one by one per row. Even if you don't have large data sets (because database programming is not just data warehouses and very large data sets), you might still have issues with performance. If the dimension of the data is moderate, what happens to your databases?

Do you know what the tragedy is? Some companies implement large data warehouse systems and deal with large data sets. These companies hire specialized database developers and these developers know how to write set-oriented code. In a data warehouse, the style is generally the proper one.

If someone tries to use the atomic approach in an ETL process, for example, the ETL will simply become almost unusable and the consequences will be detected immediately. Therefore, in a data warehouse you're less likely to find these inappropriate styles of development. However, it happens often in transactional, operational systems where people can't afford or don't think it's necessary to hire specialized database developers. In these cases, you'll usually find application developers with some SQL knowledge.

Writing Out of Habit

How does the application programmers learn the SQL language? In most cases, they learn by analogy with their application development. So style will they use? They will probably use a style similar to the atomic style of development.

Here is the logic of some IT professionals: everyone can learn SQL. It's simple. You already know Java or C#, so SQL should be a piece of cake, right? In these systems, the code can be written at the lowest level of detail. Due to the moderate dimensions of the data, the logic will not always be detected as inappropriate and the application will survive as written. The bad performance will not be so visible; the timings will be bad, but not very bad.

Choosing the lowest level of detail, the data row, and using the atomic style has another disadvantage apart from poor performance. Any bid for improvement is effectively blocked; the performance will remain very low due to the use of atomic style.

What do you do when you have low performance? You try to improve it, of course. One of the most challenging tasks for the developers is when they are instructed to improve the performance. I have been in this position many times. Do you know what I did in most of the cases? I **rewrote the entire logic!** The reason for low performance is the use of the atomic approach following the wrong decision of dealing with the lowest level of detail. If programmers choose to write their code at the row level by default, this code simply can't be optimized. All the nice features for performance, like indexes, and materialized views, are useless if the code is written in the atomic style.

Blocked into Poor Performance

Choosing to develop software at the row level and using the atomic style of development in the database has two major consequences. The performance will be very low and any improvements are impossible. **The code simply can't be optimized because all the features available for improving performance are set-oriented and not row-oriented.**

Any database system has many great facilities for improving performance. As a developer or a DBA, you need to learn to apply all of them. Unfortunately, all of these nice features are applicable for the set-oriented approach! They are almost useless if applied to the atomic style of development. So, if you want a bad performance in your database and if you want to be sure that no one can improve this performance, stay with your favorite **atomic** approach and work at the **row level** using cursors and all of the other features!

Choosing one style or another is a matter of subjective and personal experience. Experience influences and is influenced by taste. Moreover, experience and taste can be driven by the learning process. For example, I am sure many of us were not completely aware of the level of granularity, of the duality between the data set and data row, and the decision that we should always make when writing SQL. This distinction is very clear and simple, but very often we are not aware of clear and simple things.

In applications where you need to move data between systems, choosing the row level of detail is a catastrophic decision. The data movement process is like the sea. Data movement should be done in waves of data, and the waves are defined according to the business criteria. These waves of data are the data sets. Choosing the data set instead of the data row and trying to identify it whenever possible should be the principle that drives any developer when writing code in the database.

Performance Relies on a Holistic Style

One of the main tasks for an experienced database developer is the ability to read, understand, and eventually drive the execution plan of a SQL statement. The execution plan shows what the optimizer will probably choose when executing a SQL statement. Tuning SQL statements for a better performance is another critical task. Generally, the database administrators are responsible because the production environment is the real world and they are the gatekeepers. However, in reality, the SQL tuning process starts much earlier in the development environment and should be managed by the development team. First, a good database developer knows how to write clean and accurate SQL. Depending on the quantity of data to be processed, a variety of features available in any database engine will be added to the SQL statement by the database administrator. If the logic is written by an application developer who is determined to follow his favorite and familiar atomic approach, there is almost nothing to tune and almost nothing to improve!

The concept of SQL tuning implies two steps. The first step is to catch the SQL statements that seem to cause performance issues. For this, tuning tools like Oracle Enterprise Manager or SQL Server Profiler allow us to see and analyze the statements. Afterwards, we analyze all the features for performance. There are so many manuals and courses, so please refer to them if you need more information. A precondition for all of these tuning and performance features is that they are applied in a holistic style of development.

Querying … All the Time!

Although we can speak about database developers like me, most programmers are application developers. Most of the difficult work is at user interface level, and most programmers are Java, C, PHP, or C# programmers. These programmers often work at both the user interface and database level. At the user interface level, there are so many things that need to be done! However, at the relational database level, things are much simpler and straightforward. The main task of the developer is always the same: to write queries. Let's review the major tasks of a database programmer.

What Do Programmers Do?

A database programmer basically does four things:

1. The programmer reads business information. This is the **query**, the **select** statement with all the additional clauses. Let's imagine Joanna Doe again, our top programmer. She simply gets the data according to her needs. Learning how to select is very simple but it is also very difficult; this is the paradox in database programming. A query is like a business request and the set of data returned by the query is the response to the business request. A business request may be very simple or very complicated. What may be simple or complicated to the programmer is not the request itself, but the means and facilities that the programmer should use to write the select statement. One of the first things the programmer should do is identify the data set behind the request. The business request is always reflected in a data set! Being aware of this principle and thinking holistically is highly recommended.

2. The programmer may add new data via an **insert** statement. The insert can be done in classic insert-values syntax, where the values for the columns are manually supplied. The programmer may add data in a certain target from a source of data and she may use the most complex syntax, insert-select. The difficult thing is the select statement and the **set-based orientation**.

Whenever proposing to insert into a target from a source, you need to identify the source. The source of data may be taken from a table or from a variety of tables, linked by joins, and eventually grouped by union. Therefore, the difficult part in the insert statement is actually the same select statement. Again, the programmer should think **holistically** and identify the source of data as a whole. It is not always possible and, if not possible, she should move to a lower level of detail: the row.

3. The programmer, our Joanna Doe, may edit data, which means changing something. This is the **update** statement. An update can be divided in two segments. The first part is the identification of the rows to be updated. What do you want to update? The second part corresponds to the set of new values. What are the new values? When the programmer wants to see the rows to be updated, she wants to get a **data set**. Consequently, she needs to do a select statement first, the same old select statement. Secondly, she needs to find a set of data, again the same holistic vision. When she wants to find the new values, she can manually supply some values or she can get the values from a source of data. Getting the values from data sources can be very difficult; for that, again you need to build some select statements and use them to identify the sources of data for the new values.

4. The programmer can delete some data. In order to do that, she needs to identify the rows to be deleted. The programmer needs to write a select statement first (even if she does it in her mind): the select statement with the rows to be deleted. That will be, of course, another data set.

Let's look at these descriptions to find constants that occur in all four major actions. **Select** statements (the queries) should be executed all the time, before anything else. Even if a write action is required, a read action is usually correlated with it. A select statement is involved in almost everything. Secondly, a **data set is always present** in any action. You are reading and writing data sets in all of the major actions involved in database development. Dividing the data set into data rows by default is against the definitions of these major actions.

Looking at these basic actions and reviewing them, you can see the importance of the set-based approach. Even in the definition of the four important SQL statements the data set is present everywhere. The data set division, apart from the technical limitations and reasons why the division is required, is against the definitions of the major actions in database programming. What is an update? An update means changing the values for a data set. What is a delete? A delete means deleting a data set. What is an insert into a target from a source of data? This represents an insertion of a data set from a source to the target. The data set is everywhere!

How Do Programmers Do It?

When doing database development, the first task is to get the data. The only way to access data is SQL.

A database programmer needs to be able to think SQL, to think in data sets. In any programming language there are general features like variables and structures and specific features like cursors. These are part of any database developer's life. However, what is important is to realize that these facilities are not to be used before SQL.

The logic is written in stored procedures, functions, and triggers. However, when looking inside them, we should see mostly SQL. If we see a cursor, this means there was no other way for the problem to be solved in SQL.

What if you need to concatenate some values in a column, values taken from another column? You may need to position yourself in the data set, take the value from the column in a row-by-row approach, move the data into a variable, concatenate in another variable, get the result, and update the other column. This is a context where the procedural facilities of the language are required and used accordingly. Pure SQL language was not enough! This may happen, which is why you always have the cursors and the rest of procedural facilities that allow you to handle things in a row-by-row approach.

Say you need to move some data from one table to another, from a source to a target. You can think in many ways. You can declare some variables or structures, you can move the data elements into temporary storage spaces like the variables, you can open a cursor, you can move the values in the cursor and, being in the cursor, you can copy the elements from the source into the target. This is the atomic vision of the programmer. This is, in my opinion, the vision that is compatible more with typical programming, the style of programming that is described in most courses and used by most developers. The atomic vision works and the goals can be achieved. More than that, the atomic approach is followed by many application developers within the database.

The problem is that this vision, the atomic vision, is not exactly the best vision for the database. The atomic vision is not optimal and is not suitable for data.

Revisiting the SQL Shop

Let's go back to the SQL Shop. I have a basket full of products. I go to the cashier to pay for them. There are ten chocolates in the basket. Instead of paying all at once, I pay for one chocolate at a time. Obviously, a huge queue forms behind me. People in the shop get upset. I am taking too long.

The cashier hands me a bag. I look at her, very surprised. "What do you want me to do with a bag?" I ask her. The cashier stares at me. "Don't you know what these bags are for? They allow you to add many goods at one time and transport them easily. If you add the goods one by one, you don't just act illogically and against common sense, you don't just waste your time and others, but you also refuse to use the tool the right way."

So what's the main reason for this story, apart from the fact that it seems quite silly to pay for ten chocolates one at a time instead of paying for them in one shot? The reason is performance. My performance was very poor and the main consequence was the bad timing in the queues. More than that, any feature for performance improvement was useless.

In the database, using the atomic vision may not cause too much harm in the testing activity where the quantity of data is generally low and the variety of data is generally reduced. In production, however, it has a great impact. Very often, this inappropriate style may cause issues.

In my experience, whenever I was involved in performance, I almost always had to rewrite large pieces of code and replace the atomic vision with the holistic vision.

Let's go back to the example in the beginning of this section. You must move some data from one source to a destination. If you think holistically, which means SQL, you analyze the entire set of data in the source. You identify the data set to be transported into the target. For that, you need a query; that is all you need! This is actually the most difficult part. You simply take the entire set of data and move it in one shot into the target. There is no need for anything else; you don't need cursors and structures.

The Use of Scalar Functions

One valuable principle when studying languages like C or Pascal is the use of functions. Every student starts by learning the basics: variables, loops, and conditional statements. The student learns arrays and then structures. Finally the student learns functions.

Before that, everything was done in the main function. Then the student learned how to split every distinct task according to the business and how to embed it in a function.

The function can return a true value, like an integer or a string, or it can do something without returning anything, like a void function. The programmers are seduced by this principle and they keep it in their mind forever. They like how the use of functions allow them to organize their work better and to divide the complexity of their activity into less complex tasks.

The programmers build functions over functions and they remain constant to this principle of divisions: to divide the complexity and separate the task into smaller tasks embedded in functions.

After some time, the programmers starts working in the database. No one told them that working in the database is a different thing, and that they should not necessarily follow exactly the same paths and principles they use outside the database. They see that there are two main types of procedural facilities: procedures and functions. They acknowledge that a stored procedure performs an action while a function returns a value. They understand the use of a stored procedure and they see that in most cases they are doing particular actions, especially reading or writing data using the set of DML statements.

The principle of division is equally valuable and applicable in the database. However, the use of functions should be seen differently. The application programmers are accustomed to functions and they can easily see the combination between a cursor and a function. They see the **scalar function** right away as an ideal type of procedural facility for their atomic approach. A scalar function is a type of function that acts per variable, per column and row. It is the last type of function the programmers should use if they want to follow the set-based approach!

The scalar function returns a certain value of a certain type. Any scalar function can be applied to a certain column or expression in a certain row. The scalar function is the best feature for the atomic approach and it is a favorite feature of many application developers working inside the databases. Imagine you have 1,000 rows in a data set and you create one function and apply it in a cursor in the data set 1,000 times instead of avoiding that function and doing the entire logic in the data set directly! This is a very common situation in many databases!

On the other hand, in the database there are many types of functions. There are table functions that apply to data sets; these types of functions are much better than scalar functions. A good database developer should apply them directly per sets of data. That is the difference. A table function can be called per a data set while a scalar function is always called per column and row in a cursor.

A scalar function can be defined and used if you apply it to configuration tables. You know that one certain function will return one single value from a configuration table: this is the ideal scenario for a scalar function.

In the database, the main procedural object is the stored procedure. This is obvious because in the database the main task is data manipulation, either reading or writing. This is what we are doing in most of our stored procedures: reading data and writing data. Using the holistic approach and the set-based approach, we read and write data sets.

Set-Based Debugging Is Simpler

Another advantage of the holistic approach is the ease of debugging. I am referring now to **specific** systems where the goal is to move data between various systems, such as a data migration system, a replication system, or an ETL system. If such a system is built entirely in SQL, as I recommend, apart from all the advantages described in the previous pages, the debugging will be easier.

In these specific systems, you don't have the classic debug functionalities with variables and watch. There is a much simpler debug method. Whenever you have an error of a certain type, like a constraint violation or a conversion error, there is an error handling procedure that shows you the place where the error occurred. It is very simple. All you need to do is to simulate everything until that point; you need to make sure you have the data when the error occurs. You take the entire set of data separately, check the data, and see what caused the error.

In most cases, the reason for the error will be a data set. Take that data set, analyze it, and figure out which details of the data set caused the error.

If the migration system is properly organized in steps, if the error handling procedure is built coherently, then it can catch the error and store it in the error table. There you can see the step and the error identifier and description. There could be constraint violations errors or conversion errors. You simply comment the steps after the step with the error and run the interface until that point. You then take the step with the error and check the data. You query the data before the error, analyze it, and see what caused it. Again, for debugging, SQL is the required skill. In order to be able to identify the reasons for the error, you need to query the data and see what was happening. It is very straightforward!

Another advantage of the holistic approach is readability. The code is much clearer, and you can see everything organized in data sets.

Your Role as a Database Developer

I want to add some words about database development. Let's look at the market. Database development is an accepted specialization nowadays, after many years when mainly database administrators were accepted as distinct database specialists. Now there is an explosion of database specialists and a continuous and increasing demand. This change is because more and more reporting and analytics databases are being built over the set of operational systems everywhere.

Data warehouse and big data technologies are more and present everywhere. The BI technologies are increasingly more popular in the market. Database developers (along with business analysts and reporting analysts) are the ones that can sustain all these increasing demands.

However, from my perspective as a SQL developer and specialist, despite appearances things are not very different today. SQL is still considered in the "other" section for many projects and many teams. Let's analyze the specialized PL/SQL developers who use the atomic approach and the procedural facilities. They call themselves as database developers. I call them application developers, because they do not think SQL and holistically, even though they are developing in PL/SQL.

In the field of data warehousing where there are so many ETL systems, and in medium or large companies with a variety of systems communicating between them by specific replication systems or data migration systems, more and more database developers are needed. The set-oriented approach is requested on the market, and this shows that the enterprises are aware of the necessity of the holistic approach. The project managers should either decide to use specialized database developers or teach application developers to write holistically.

Practice Time!

Finally, after so much discussions, concepts, and clarifications, it is time for some exercises. In the following chapters, I will illustrate the two styles of development with examples. I will show that the holistic approach is the best approach when in the database.

As mentioned, the examples are taken from two major database management systems, Oracle and SQL Server. I want to reaffirm that all the considerations and thoughts described in this book are general and refer to any relational database system. The holistic approach is a vision that should be present in any relational database. These examples can be easily reproduced in any other database system.

It will be very easy for you to translate the holistic version because SQL is a standard and the syntax is very similar. In the atomic approach, you will have to work to translate the examples from Oracle or SQL Server to your system. The procedural languages are similar but there are differences; there is no standard, apart from the same mode of structured programing.

CHAPTER 5

■ ■ ■

Data Transfer Paradigm

Starting with this chapter, I will demonstrate the two styles through a variety of examples. These examples will make the distinctions very clear. My main goal in this book is to clarify the two styles of development, to show the differences between them, and to show the advantages and disadvantages of each. I also intend to promote the holistic style. Please feel free to experiment with applying the two styles.

About the Examples

The considerations and the arguments for a certain style of programming specific to the database versus a classic style specific to the user interface will be illustrated in the following chapters via a list of practices and exercises. These examples will explain the two approaches, the holistic approach and the atomic approach. The purpose is to show that, inside a relational database, the holistic approach should be used in most cases.

I have organized the examples so they can be compared and tested on your own systems. I invite you to run the exercises and see the differences for yourself. I recommend that you create a distinct user and schema for the exercises; for example, I call it two_styles. Add all the developer privileges like create table, for example. Execute the scripts under this user.

Of course, the ideal is to imagine similar practices in your systems and test one approach versus another in your logic inside your databases. Even more ideal is to change your style in the systems you are working on at this moment, if that applies to you. The best way to see the differences is by analyzing real data and real scenarios.

Take these examples and practices as what they are: some simple exercises. This means you don't need to focus on the examples, which are actually trivial examples, but on the way the problems are solved and the style of programming that drives the solutions. Despite the simplicity of the exercises, the style of development behind the scenes is the same (one or another or a mixture of both).

The most important things have been already said in the previous chapters; the main ideas have even been repeated many times. These examples will just reinforce and confirm the statements, advice, and ideas expressed in the first part of this book.

One of the most important characteristic of an exercise or practice is the **context**. The context of an example consists of the **business description** of the exercise, the technical description that should be generated from the business description, the characteristics and prerequisites of the sample, like the data definition statements that

© Stefan Ardeleanu 2016
S. Ardeleanu, *Relational Database Programming*, DOI 10.1007/978-1-4842-2080-1_5

may be used for the exercise, and the goals that need to be achieved in each example. I don't focus too much on the business description.

Most of the exercises are illustrated in both Oracle and SQL Server, more precisely in both PL SQL and Transact SQL. Almost all of the principles and almost all of the examples can be reproduced similarly in any other database system, like IBM DB2, PostgreSQL, Sybase and others. Oracle and SQL Server are the systems I chose to show the relevant examples because they are popular systems; that's all! These principles are not specific to these two popular database management systems; they are common to all of them.

Please take note again of the fact that the goal is to illustrate a holistic approach in a relational database system.

Format of the Examples

Most examples in this and later chapters contain similar elements and follow a common pattern. Examples are introduced in the context of a business problem. Then I provide a technical description. Each example contains a set of data definition language statements (DDL) associated with it, like a list of prerequisites or a list of the tables involved.

In most cases, the DDL used in the examples is associated with a sample of data, enough to illustrate my points. The business description is very important and I will define the purposes and the goals with enough clarity so that the examples can be clearly understood. The solutions are driven from these business descriptions and I show how the business description can be the key to one style of development or another.

I illustrate and describe the various methods that are used, and the explanations and reasons for choosing one technique or another. This is maybe the most important part because here the reader can see and understand one style of development or another.

I display the scripts in Oracle, SQL Server, or both. These scripts will sometimes be embedded in stored procedures because they are the most representative type of object in database programming.

I always compare the two approaches because the purpose of these examples is to compare and describe the advantages or disadvantages of one style of development or another. I admit that the purpose of most of the exercises is to promote the holistic, set-oriented style specific to database developers versus the atomic and row-oriented style specific to application developers.

In most cases, if you want to practice on your own, you can execute the two examples in Oracle or SQL Server, or whatever system you prefer, and compare the results.

Example 1: A Full Data Transfer Between Two Systems

Very often, when doing database development, we are simply transferring data between a source and a target. By transferring data, I mean moving data from A to B, eventually updating or deleting information based on certain conditions. The process of **data transfer** can be made in any kind of application: a classic application or a specific application. It is one of the most common operations in database programming. Very often, programming paradigms are quite simple, and database development is one good example that confirms this statement. In most cases, we are doing pretty much the same thing, and the data transfer paradigm is one of the first tasks for anyone working in a relational database.

To illustrate some data transfer examples, I chose a simple model. Imagine moving data between two systems. The first system is a normalized system and the second one is a reporting or analytic system where a certain degree of normalization may exist.

A data transfer can be **full** or **incremental**. I consider a transfer a full one if the target is completely deleted before the transfer. An incremental transfer is committed when the data is moved incrementally and only the changes from the source system are applied to the target.

This first example will illustrate a full transfer. The second example will show an incremental data transfer, which is a more complex scenario.

Let's define the context. It will be the base for most of the examples that follow.

Business and Technical Description

The **context** specifies the source and target systems. A set of countries, languages, and their association is part of the source system, and a set of reporting tables per language is part of the destination system. The source system (named A) contains a set of three tables to store the following information:

1. A list of countries

2. A list of languages

3. The association between countries and languages, including some common information for both country and language

The target system (named B) may be a separate system or not. Let's consider it a separate reporting system where the data is denormalized according to the language. The system contains a list of tables per language with country information.

There is one table for the English language and one for the French language. The target system contains a list of reporting tables per language. (For simplicity, I'm using just the English and French languages because this is enough to illustrate my goals.)

The information from the source system, A, should be moved into the destination system, B. The goal is to generate the set of countries for the English language in the specific table containing only the English countries and, eventually, the set of countries for French language in the specific table containing the French countries.

Prerequisites

Let's continue with the context definition. You just saw the business and technical description of the context. Now let's see the table design. The source system, A, is composed of three tables, shown in Listing 5-1.

Listing 5-1. Countries and Languages Design

```
CREATE TABLE Countries
(
Country_Id INT CONSTRAINT  NN_Country_Id NOT NULL,
Country_Code VARCHAR(3) CONSTRAINT  NN_Country_Code NOT NULL,
Country_Name VARCHAR(50) CONSTRAINT  NN_Country_Name NOT NULL,
Continent VARCHAR(15) CONSTRAINT  NN_Country_Continent
NOT NULL,
CONSTRAINT  PK_Country_Id PRIMARY KEY (Country_Id),
CONSTRAINT  UQ_Country_Code UNIQUE (Country_Code),
CONSTRAINT  CK_Country_Continent
CHECK(Continent IN ('Europe', 'North America' ,'South America', 'Asia',
'Africa', 'Australia', 'Central America'))
);

CREATE TABLE Languages
(
        Language_Id INT CONSTRAINT  NN_Language_Id NOT NULL,
        Language_Name VARCHAR(50)
CONSTRAINT  NN_Language_Name NOT NULL,
        CONSTRAINT  PK_Language_Id PRIMARY KEY (Language_Id),
        CONSTRAINT  UQ_Language_Name UNIQUE (Language_Name)
);
CREATE TABLE Countries_Languages
(
        CL_Id INT CONSTRAINT  NN_CL_Id NOT NULL,
        Language_Id INT CONSTRAINT  NN_CL_Language_Id NOT NULL,
        Country_Id INT CONSTRAINT  NN_CL_Country_Id NOT NULL,
        Language_Category VARCHAR(10)
CONSTRAINT  NN_CL_Category NOT NULL,
        Make_Flag INT,
        CONSTRAINT  PK_CL_Id PRIMARY KEY (CL_Id),
        CONSTRAINT  UQ_Language_Country
UNIQUE (Language_Id, Country_Id),
        CONSTRAINT  CK_CL_Category
CHECK (Language_Category IN ('MAIN', 'SECONDARY')),
        CONSTRAINT  CK_CL_Make_Flag CHECK (Make_Flag IN (0, 1)),
        CONSTRAINT  FK_CL_Countries
FOREIGN KEY (Country_Id) REFERENCES Countries(Country_Id),
        CONSTRAINT  FK_CL_Languages
FOREIGN KEY (Language_Id) REFERENCES Languages (Language_Id)
);
-- Build an Oracle sequence too
CREATE SEQUENCE CL_Id_Seq;
```

Create these objects in Oracle, SQL Server, or both if you want to reproduce the examples yourself.

According to the design in Listing 5-1, there is one table for the countries, one for the languages, and one for the association between the countries and the languages. According to the business needs, some languages should be associated with some countries and some common information will be added there.

I want to review some of the design considerations shown in this script.

1. Notice that every table has its own primary key, as it should be in a normalized system. The primary key is enforced by an artificial column with no business meaning. This is the most common scenario. I always prefer to keep the primary key away from the business.

2. Sometimes, when the primary key is artificial, you can add a unique constraint. This is the so-called unique business key and it defines the table from the business point of view. For example, the code of the country should be unique and that code has a business meaning, compared to the artificial key with the sole purpose of uniquely identifying one row. The combination language and country should also be unique in the association table, so you can see the unique constraint. The business key can be defined as the primary key. Technically speaking, it's a suitable candidate, but I prefer to separate things and to always keep the primary key away from the business.

3. The constraints are all named constraints, not system generated. The names are very relevant and are generally obtained by the concatenation between the table, column, and constraint type. The names can be seen in the set of system objects or data dictionary, so the developer can quickly understand what's going on by the names. The constraint names are also visible in error messages so the developer can quickly see what the errors refer to. I recommend that the prefix of the constraint be the constraint type.

4. Add the check constraints or foreign key constraints whenever possible. If you know the exact values, do not hesitate and do not leave the columns optional. Combine the check constraints with **NOT NULL** constraints. In most cases, a column with low selectivity can have a check constraint. See if that is the case and add both constraints, if possible. If the list with values defined by the check constraint will increase in time, you should transform the check constraint into a foreign key constraint. Add a lookup table first and restrict the table using that lookup table. Before choosing the type of constraint, think of the future. Although there may only be a few values now, if you anticipate that the list may grow, add the lookup table from the beginning.

5. It is good to apply the constraints and to restrict the data to be conformed to the business definition. If the layer of constraints is properly set from the beginning, you have a good starting point in your database development activity. You can see in the example that almost every column has at least one constraint attached to it. Of course, descriptive fields won't have any constraints. However, the tip is to see if any type of constraint can be applied in one way or another to the column and do this investigation constantly for any column in any table.

6. You can see that this script can be executed as is in Oracle and SQL Server and in others database systems too. This is the advantage of the standard!

Let's now illustrate the destination system. The target system, B, is composed of a list of reporting tables per country. You can see these tables in Listing 5-2.

Listing 5-2. The Destination System Design

```
CREATE TABLE English_European_Countries
(
        English_CL_Id INT CONSTRAINT  NN_English_CL_Id NOT NULL,
        Country_Code VARCHAR(3)
CONSTRAINT  NN_LCountry_Code NOT NULL,
        Country_Name VARCHAR(50)
CONSTRAINT  NN_LCountry_Name NOT NULL,
        Language_Category VARCHAR(10),
        CONSTRAINT  PK_English_CL_Id PRIMARY KEY (English_CL_Id),
        CONSTRAINT  UQ_ECountry_Code_Category
UNIQUE (Country_Code, Language_Category));
CREATE TABLE French_European_Countries
(
        French_CL_Id INT CONSTRAINT  NN_French_CL_Id NOT NULL,
        Country_Code VARCHAR(3)
CONSTRAINT  NN_FCountry_Code NOT NULL,
        Country_Name VARCHAR(50)
CONSTRAINT  NN_FCountry_Name NOT NULL,
        Language_Category VARCHAR(10),
        CONSTRAINT  PK_French_CL_Id PRIMARY KEY (French_CL_Id),
        CONSTRAINT  UQ_FCountry_Code_Category
UNIQUE (Country_Code, Language_Category)
);
Other reporting tables may be added per various languages.
```

Here is reporting activity where the reports are set per language and the data is divided per language. The examples want to illustrate a style, and this style is recommended for databases in general, but specifically for a replication system, a data migration system, or a data warehouse system.

Sample of the Data

Let's see the initial data. It will be used in most of the examples in this book. For anyone working in databases, such as programmers, analysts, or testers, the data should have a strong relevancy. The business reflects in the data. Any database design should be associated with some samplings.

Table 5-1 lists counties, Table 5-2 contains a sampling of languages, and Table 5-3 contains some common data in an association table. The data is highly normalized and will implement a many-to-many relationship between countries and languages, which is the reason for the association table, Countries_Languages (see the design in Listing 5-1).

Table 5-1. *Sample Country Values*

Country ID	Code	Name	Continent
1	AR	Argentina	South America
2	AT	Austria	Europe
3	FR	France	Europe
4	MT	Malta	Europe
5	ES	Spain	Europe
6	CH	Switzerland	Europe
7	NL	The Netherlands	Europe
8	UK	United Kingdom	Europe
9	US	United States of America	North America

Table 5-2. *Sample Language Values*

Language ID	Language Name
1	Dutch
2	English
3	French
4	German
5	Maltese
6	Spanish

Table 5-3. *Countries and Languages*

Id	Language Id	Country Id	Category	Make Flag
1	6	1	MAIN	0
2	4	2	MAIN	1
3	3	3	MAIN	1
4	2	4	MAIN	1
5	5	4	MAIN	0
6	6	5	MAIN	NULL
7	3	6	MAIN	1
8	4	6	MAIN	0
9	2	6	SECONDARY	1
10	1	7	MAIN	1
11	2	7	SECONDARY	0
12	2	8	MAIN	1
13	2	9	MAIN	0

An Example Insert Script

Before starting the first example, due to the fact that most of the exercises will be taken from these samplings of countries and languages, let's discuss the insert script, so anyone who wants to do so can effectively execute all the examples and reproduce the exact conditions as in my system.

Listing 5-3 shows the INSERT statements used to put the example data from Tables 5-1 through 5-3 into the example tables. The countries, languages, and their associations are initialized with the required quantity of data. The tables above show this initial data. Now the same data can be seen in a more technical manner, in an insert script. Of course, if execute the insert script in Oracle, don't forget to commit!

Listing 5-3. Insert Script to Populate Countries and Languages

```
INSERT INTO Countries (Country_Id, Country_Code, Country_Name, Continent)
VALUES (1, 'AR', 'Argentina', 'South America');
INSERT INTO Countries (Country_Id, Country_Code, Country_Name, Continent)
VALUES (2, 'AT', 'Austria', 'Europe');
INSERT INTO Countries (Country_Id, Country_Code, Country_Name, Continent)
VALUES (3, 'FR', 'France', 'Europe');
INSERT INTO Countries (Country_Id, Country_Code, Country_Name, Continent)
VALUES (4, 'MT', 'Malta', 'Europe');
INSERT INTO Countries (Country_Id, Country_Code, Country_Name, Continent)
VALUES (5, 'ES', 'Spain', 'Europe');
INSERT INTO Countries (Country_Id, Country_Code, Country_Name, Continent)
VALUES (6, 'CH', 'Switzerland', 'Europe');
```

```
INSERT INTO Countries (Country_Id, Country_Code, Country_Name, Continent)
VALUES (7, 'NL', 'The Netherlands', 'Europe');
INSERT INTO Countries (Country_Id, Country_Code, Country_Name, Continent)
VALUES (8, 'UK', 'United Kingdom', 'Europe');
INSERT INTO Countries (Country_Id, Country_Code, Country_Name, Continent)
VALUES (9, 'US', 'United States of America', 'North America');
INSERT INTO Languages (Language_Id, Language_Name) VALUES (1, 'Dutch');
INSERT INTO Languages (Language_Id, Language_Name) VALUES (2, 'English');
INSERT INTO Languages (Language_Id, Language_Name) VALUES (3, 'French');
INSERT INTO Languages (Language_Id, Language_Name) VALUES (4, 'German');
INSERT INTO Languages (Language_Id, Language_Name) VALUES (5, 'Maltese');
INSERT INTO Languages (Language_Id, Language_Name) VALUES (6, 'Spanish');
INSERT INTO Countries_Languages (CL_Id, Country_Id, Language_Id,
Language_Category, Make_Flag) VALUES (1, 1, 6, 'MAIN', 0);
INSERT INTO Countries_Languages (CL_Id, Country_Id, Language_Id,
Language_Category, Make_Flag) VALUES (2, 2, 4, 'MAIN', 1);
INSERT INTO Countries_Languages (CL_Id, Country_Id, Language_Id,
Language_Category, Make_Flag) VALUES (3, 3, 3, 'MAIN', 1);
INSERT INTO Countries_Languages (CL_Id, Country_Id, Language_Id,
Language_Category, Make_Flag) VALUES (4, 4, 2, 'MAIN', 1);
INSERT INTO Countries_Languages (CL_Id, Country_Id, Language_Id,
Language_Category, Make_Flag) VALUES (5, 4, 5, 'MAIN', 0);
INSERT INTO Countries_Languages (CL_Id, Country_Id, Language_Id,
Language_Category, Make_Flag) VALUES (6, 5, 6, 'MAIN', NULL);
INSERT INTO Countries_Languages (CL_Id, Country_Id, Language_Id,
Language_Category, Make_Flag) VALUES (7, 6, 3, 'MAIN', 1);
INSERT INTO Countries_Languages (CL_Id, Country_Id, Language_Id,
Language_Category, Make_Flag) VALUES (8, 6, 4, 'MAIN', 0);
INSERT INTO Countries_Languages (CL_Id, Country_Id, Language_Id,
Language_Category, Make_Flag) VALUES (9, 6, 2, 'SECONDARY', 1);
INSERT INTO Countries_Languages (CL_Id, Country_Id, Language_Id,
Language_Category, Make_Flag) VALUES (10, 7, 1, 'MAIN', 1);
INSERT INTO Countries_Languages (CL_Id, Country_Id, Language_Id,
Language_Category, Make_Flag) VALUES (11, 7, 2, 'SECONDARY', 0);
INSERT INTO Countries_Languages (CL_Id, Country_Id, Language_Id,
Language_Category, Make_Flag) VALUES (12, 8, 2, 'MAIN', 1);
INSERT INTO Countries_Languages (CL_Id, Country_Id, Language_Id,
Language_Category, Make_Flag) VALUES (13, 9, 2, 'MAIN', 0);
```

Filtering for English and French

Listing 5-4 shows the atomic solution to the problem as implemented in Oracle. This is the row-by-row solution that in my experience will be chosen by many application developers.

Listing 5-4. Full Data Transfer, Atomic Style, Using Oracle

```
CREATE PROCEDURE Atomic_Full_Transfer_Country
(p_Language_Name VARCHAR)
AS
  v_Country_Name VARCHAR2(50);
  v_Country_Code VARCHAR2(3);
  v_Language_Category VARCHAR2(10);
  v_New_EEC_Id INT;
  CURSOR c_Get_Countries (p_Language VARCHAR2) IS
  SELECT c.Country_Name, c.Country_Code, cl.Language_Category
  FROM Countries_Languages cl INNER JOIN Languages l
          ON (l.Language_Id = cl.Language_Id)
  INNER JOIN Countries c
          ON (c.Country_Id = cl.Country_Id)
  WHERE l.Language_Name = p_Language;
BEGIN
  v_New_EEC_Id := 1;
  IF p_Language_Name = 'English' THEN
          DELETE English_European_Countries;
  ELSIF p_Language_Name = 'French' THEN
  DELETE French_European_Countries;
  END IF;
  OPEN c_Get_Countries (p_Language_Name);
  LOOP
    FETCH c_Get_Countries
          INTO v_Country_Name, v_Country_Code, v_Language_Category;
    EXIT WHEN c_Get_Countries%NOTFOUND;
        IF p_Language_Name = 'English' THEN
                INSERT INTO English_European_Countries (English_CL_Id,
                Country_Code, Country_Name, Language_Category)
                VALUES (v_New_EEC_Id, v_Country_Code, v_Country_Name,
                v_Language_Category);
        ELSIF p_Language_Name = 'French' THEN
                INSERT INTO French_European_Countries (French_CL_Id,
                Country_Code, Country_Name, Language_Category)
                VALUES (v_New_EEC_Id, v_Country_Code, v_Country_Name,
                v_Language_Category);
        END IF;
  v_New_EEC_Id := v_New_EEC_Id + 1;
  COMMIT;
  END LOOP;
  CLOSE c_Get_Countries;
END Atomic_Full_Transfer_Country;
/
```

You can see from Table 5-1 (Countries) that there is a list of countries with an artificial identifier, a name, a unique code, and the continent. Looking at Table 5-2 (Languages) you can see the artificial identifier and the name of the language. The association table (Table 5-3) has one language and one country, like any association table. Apart from that, the category of a language can be MAIN or SECONDARY for the country and there is a flag for each country language combination. The destination table has another artificial identifier as primary key, the country code, name, and the category. You are positioned in the English or French language so you know that you are within a certain language. This is why no language reference is required, just the country information.

The task is to fill the reporting table, either the English or French one, from the set of normalized tables. The transfer is a full transfer because the target table with countries is first deleted. Let's analyze the Oracle version.

Listing 5-4 shows the first solution using the atomic approach and the associated style of development. Just to clarify, even though the details should be straightforward, I will describe the flow for this first example.

1.   The parameter is the language, either French or English. The list may expand for others languages, of course.

2.   You declare some variables to store the data to be inserted, for country name and code, for the language category, and for the key identifier that should be generated. Obviously, you can use a record or structure instead of the variables to achieve the same goal. The purpose is to be able to store atomically the values to be inserted in these variables. You can already see how code is atomically oriented: you are preparing to store the data and manipulate it at the atomic (row) level.

3.   You declare the cursor that will store the country name, code, and the language category from the series of source tables (Countries, Languages, Countries_ Languages). The cursor with the loop facility, which allows you to position it wherever you want it in the data set, is the base for the atomic approach.

4.   You initialize the value for the identifier to 1, using the dedicated variable v_New_EEC_Id. The primary key from the target, an artificial identifier, will have to receive a unique value taken from this variable.

5.   Based on the language, either English or French, the logic deletes one reporting table or another. The transfer is full so the target table is deleted first.

6.   You open the cursor and start adding the values from the cursor into the variables using the fetch instruction. This is the classic series of steps in every cursor.

7. Based on the language, the data is added into the target table, row by row. For every row, the data is inserted from the variables that store the current set of values from the cursor. The same if-else statement is used to detect the target table based on the language.

8. You increment the key to prepare the next value for the next iteration.

9. This procedural style corresponds to the atomic approach of programming. Many application developers think atomically in almost any circumstance; they try to use the same style in the database that they use in the user interface. They know the principles of structured programming and they apply them here at the row level.

Let's see the results for both countries. After executing in Oracle the procedure specified in Listing 5-4, with the parameter English (EXECUTE Atomic_Full_Transfer_Country ('English'), you need to query from the reporting table English_European_Countries. Change the parameter to French and query the second reporting table. Tables 5-4 and 5-5 show the rows that will be transferred between systems.

Table 5-4. *Rows transferred, English*

English CL Id	Country Code	Country Name	Country Category
1	MT	Malta	MAIN
2	CH	Switzerland	SECONDARY
3	NL	The Netherlands	SECONDARY
4	UK	United Kingdom	MAIN
5	US	United States of America	MAIN

Table 5-5. *Rows transferred, French*

French CL Id	Country Code	Country Name	Country Category
1	FR	France	MAIN
2	CH	Switzerland	MAIN

Before continuing to comment on this approach, let's see the SQL Server version of the atomic approach. You can see it in Listing 5-5. You see all the same steps. This should demonstrate the classic, procedural, and atomic style of development. Move the data into the variables one by one and populate the table with new rows one by one, according to the values stored in the variables.

Listing 5-5. Full Data Transfer, Atomic Style, in SQL Server

```
CREATE PROCEDURE Atomic_Full_Transfer_Country
(
 @p_Language_Name VARCHAR(50)
)
AS
  DECLARE @v_Country_Name VARCHAR(50);
  DECLARE @v_Country_Code VARCHAR(3);
  DECLARE @v_Language_Category VARCHAR(10);
  DECLARE @v_New_EEC_Id INT;
  DECLARE c_Get_Countries CURSOR FOR
  SELECT c.Country_Name, c.Country_Code, cl.Language_Category
  FROM Countries_Languages cl INNER JOIN Languages l
              ON (l.Language_Id = cl.Language_Id)
  INNER JOIN Countries c
              ON (c.Country_Id = cl.Country_Id)
  WHERE UPPER(l.Language_Name) = UPPER(@p_Language_Name);
BEGIN
        SET @v_New_EEC_Id = 1;
        IF @p_Language_Name = 'English'
              DELETE English_European_Countries;
        ELSE IF @p_Language_Name = 'French'
              DELETE French_European_Countries;
        OPEN c_Get_Countries
        FETCH NEXT FROM c_Get_Countries
        INTO @v_Country_Name, @v_Country_Code, @v_Language_Category;
        WHILE (@@FETCH_STATUS = 0)
        BEGIN
                IF @p_Language_Name = 'English'
                        INSERT INTO English_European_Countries (English_CL_Id,
                        Country_Code, Country_Name, Language_Category)
                        VALUES (@v_New_EEC_Id, @v_Country_Code, @v_Country_
                        Name, @v_Language_Category);
                ELSE IF @p_Language_Name = 'French'
                        INSERT INTO French_European_Countries (French_CL_Id,
                        Country_Code, Country_Name, Language_Category)
                        VALUES (@v_New_EEC_Id, @v_Country_Code, @v_Country_
                        Name, @v_Language_Category);
                SET @v_New_EEC_Id = @v_New_EEC_Id + 1;
        FETCH NEXT FROM c_Get_Countries INTO @v_Country_Name, @v_Country_
        Code, @v_Language_Category;
        END
  CLOSE c_Get_Countries;
  DEALLOCATE c_Get_Countries;
END;
GO
```

65

Execute the procedure with the values for the parameters of English and then French, and check the reporting tables in SQL Server. You will get the same results as in Oracle, of course.

Notice how the data is manipulated atomically and procedurally, row by row. These programmers completely exclude the holistic manipulation of the data set from their logic. They may be aware of the data set because the query that defines the cursor is the data set. However, the application developers think that the data row is the only thing they should take into consideration when writing their logic. They do not try to analyze and they do not question if they can solve the problem in a holistic manner; they are prepared by default to divide everything in rows, at the lowest level of detail. This style of development is a consequence of their classic and typical vision of programming and of their decision to ignore the fact that they are now developing in a specific, data-oriented environment, where the concept of data set should be incorporated into their structured model of programming.

It is true that sometimes we need to solve things atomically. There are business and technical situations where division is required because some problems cannot be simply solved at the data set level. Still, most tasks can be solved by affecting everything as a whole and not piece by piece or row by row. Consider a replication system or a data migration system, that type of application I was talking about earlier. Imagine you are moving medium-to-large quantities of data from different sources to different targets and imagine you are following the atomic approach. The first thing to suffer will be the performance. You can add thousands of indexes; you can do whatever you want, but you won't solve the issue. The issue is the improper style of programming.

Now let's look at the holistic, SQL approach for the same example. Listing 5-6 shows the set-based solution in Oracle. Notice the differences in terms of readability and simplicity. See how clear the code is in the holistic approach compared to the code in the atomic approach.

Listing 5-6. Full Data Transfer, Holistic Style, in Oracle

```
CREATE PROCEDURE Holistic_Full_Transf_Country
(
  p_Language_Name VARCHAR
)
AS
BEGIN
        DELETE English_European_Countries
        WHERE p_Language_Name = 'English';
        DELETE French_European_Countries
        WHERE p_Language_Name = 'French';
  INSERT INTO English_European_Countries (English_CL_Id, Country_Code,
  Country_Name, Language_Category)
        SELECT ROW_NUMBER() OVER (ORDER BY c.Country_Code, cl.Language_
        Category) AS English_CL_Id, c.Country_Code,
        c.Country_Name, cl.Language_Category
        FROM Countries_Languages cl INNER JOIN Languages l
                ON (l.Language_Id = cl.Language_Id)
```

```
        INNER JOIN Countries c
                ON (c.Country_Id = cl.Country_Id)
        WHERE l.Language_Name = p_Language_Name
AND p_Language_Name = 'English';
    INSERT INTO French_European_Countries (French_CL_Id, Country_Code,
    Country_Name, Language_Category)
        SELECT ROW_NUMBER() OVER (ORDER BY c.Country_Code, cl.Language_
        Category) AS French_CL_Id, c.Country_Code,
        c.Country_Name, cl.Language_Category
        FROM Countries_Languages cl INNER JOIN Languages l
                ON (l.Language_Id = cl.Language_Id)
        INNER JOIN Countries c
                ON (c.Country_Id = cl.Country_Id)
        WHERE l.Language_Name = p_Language_Name
AND p_Language_Name = 'French';
        COMMIT;
END Holistic_Full_Transf_Country;
/
```

This Oracle stored procedure contains only SQL statements, no procedural instructions. The stored procedure contains two delete statements and two insert statements and that's it! The logic moves the data in data sets (in waves, as I like to say). The entire transfer is seen as one transfer and there was no need for any movement at the row level.

Now let's see the SQL Server version of the holistic approach and then analyze the holistic approach in greater detail. Listing 5-7 shows the SQL Server solution.

Listing 5-7. Full Data Transfer, Holistic Style, in SQL Server

```
CREATE PROCEDURE Holistic_Full_Transf_Country
(
  @p_Language_Name VARCHAR(50)
)
AS
BEGIN
        DELETE English_European_Countries
        WHERE @p_Language_Name = 'English';
        DELETE French_European_Countries
        WHERE @p_Language_Name = 'French';
    INSERT INTO English_European_Countries (English_CL_Id, Country_Code,
    Country_Name, Language_Category)
        SELECT ROW_NUMBER() OVER (ORDER BY c.Country_Code, cl.Language_
        Category) AS English_CL_Id,
        c.Country_Code, c.Country_Name, cl.Language_Category
        FROM Countries_Languages cl INNER JOIN Languages l
                ON (l.Language_Id = cl.Language_Id)
        INNER JOIN Countries c
                ON (c.Country_Id = cl.Country_Id)
        WHERE l.Language_Name = @p_Language_Name
```

```
AND @p_Language_Name = 'English';
    INSERT INTO French_European_Countries (French_CL_Id, Country_Code,
    Country_Name, Language_Category)
        SELECT ROW_NUMBER() OVER (ORDER BY c.Country_Code, cl.Language_
        Category) AS French_CL_Id,
        c.Country_Code, c.Country_Name, cl.Language_Category
        FROM Countries_Languages cl INNER JOIN Languages l
                ON (l.Language_Id = cl.Language_Id)
        INNER JOIN Countries c
                ON (c.Country_Id = cl.Country_Id)
        WHERE l.Language_Name = @p_Language_Name
AND @p_Language_Name = 'French';
END
GO
```

Execute the procedures in either Oracle or SQL Server and check the results. Compare the results of the holistic approach with the results of the atomic approach to make sure you have the same results. The goal was achieved in both cases, but the method and style are different.

Let's analyze the steps, as we did for the atomic versions. Here's how the holistic solutions operate:

1. Delete the table with English or French languages, based on the parameter's value. The deletion is holistic: all the countries for the respective language are deleted.

2. Insert the English or French countries, based on the value of the parameter, in one single instruction: all the countries for the respective languages are added and the new identifier is generated using the function Row_Number. Both steps are set-based and holistic. Whether its 2 countries, 10 countries, or 1,000 countries, all of them are added in one single statement. There is one set of countries. You don't care how many are within the data set; you visualize the set of countries and you don't care about the details.

I believe the difference in terms of simplicity is obvious. There are merely two steps, and they are simple steps. In contrast, the atomic approach required nine steps; it is clearly more complex to grasp.

In terms of portability, things should be clear now with this example. The only difference between Oracle and SQL Server is the naming convention for variables: in SQL Server the @ sign is required! The portability advantage clearly goes to the holistic, set-based approach.

The versions of stored procedures are almost identical! You need to know the specific syntax for SQL Server, which is the declarative language of Transact SQL or you need to know the procedural language for Oracle, which is PL SQL. These procedural languages are similar in some aspects. There is no standard, just the same principles of structured programming. It's not hard to learn a new programming database language, especially when you know another one, but it does take some time. For the holistic approach, things are much simpler. The standard is followed by all vendors inside their programming languages. The SQL from SQL Server and the SQL from Oracle are almost the same. The slight differences may be accommodated easily.

Try It on Your Own

Dear reader, I encourage you to solve similar exercises in both ways! Please identify a data set and affect it in a holistic manner. Then divide the data set into rows, use cursors, and complete the task using the atomic and procedural approach. Apart from the fact that the code looks so different, and apart from the increased complexity of the procedural approach, in most cases you will notice increased performance from the holistic approach when operating on medium-to-large quantities of data. You will not see a big difference in performance for just two to three rows, but you will notice a difference as the number of rows increases.

You need to check the results after the execution in the atomic approach, save the results, go back to the starting conditions, and then implement the solution using the holistic approach. Compare the results and, if there are differences, try to see why. If the logic is well written, there should be no differences.

After you make sure that the result sets are correct, you may check the performance. I was not able to see many cases where the performance in the database suffered due to the holistic approach versus the atomic approach.

Of course, using the holistic approach, even the SQL itself can be improved. Writing SQL instead of writing procedurally is the first condition for good performance. The second condition is knowing how to write the **best** SQL. A good database developer will take the SQL and rewrite it repeatedly until he has the best code. Then he can apply additional features like indexes, materialized views in a static environment like a data warehouse, and so many others. All these performance facilities are useless if they are applied to the atomic and procedural code. The atomic and procedural code itself will generate a poor performance.

Some Conclusions

No one should write atomically in the relational database. If you analyze the holistic approach and compare it with the atomic approach, you will see how the degree of simplicity is obviously in favor of the holistic approach. If you are an application developer, I am asking you to be objective and to free yourself from your paradigms and models.

In the holistic approach, you can see how the procedural code was completely avoided: even the `if-else` was excluded from the logic! I removed the `if-else` and replaced it with the condition for the parameter to be English or French; my goal was to minimize the use of procedural code completely. In a replication system written in SQL, an ETL or a data migration system, this is a great advantage in terms of performance. The data movement is done in data sets, which is the fastest possible way!

Working based on sets, holistically, and in SQL is the most suitable style within a relational database. It is the authentic style of a database developer.

Building a specific data migration system in the holistic manner requires having good SQL professionals with a perfect understanding of the data. This means having a good understanding of the concept of a data set. Some developers that think SQL is the most valuable asset in this context. I believe that very often the use of tools can be avoided.

Example 2: Incrementally Update a Target

The first example was relatively easy. This is the general rule: one should always start with a simple example. Let's increase the complexity and see more examples to illustrate the two styles of programming.

You just saw one feature that works with the set-based approach: the row number function. Apart from the simple copy example, one other requirement was to dynamically generate an artificial identifier for the key in the target. The tendency of the application developer is clear: they believe that they need to manipulate data row by row to generate the artificial identifier. They don't know that the database system has a set of operators and functions dedicated to set-based approach that will allow them to avoid the row-by-row data manipulation.

Let's continue using the same design. You are in the same data migration system and you are moving data from a production system, where all the countries and languages are stored in one place, into a destination system where the data is organized per language. Let's increase the complexity of the data transfer and assume that the data is not completely erased before the transfer. The data transfer will be **incremental**, so only the changes will be applied to the target.

Changes to the Source

Three changes will occur in the source tables. For Malta, the English language will become a secondary language instead of the principal one (MAIN). You completely delete the English language from Switzerland, and you add the English language as a secondary language for Austria. You also add a new country, Algeria, along with a new language, Algerian Arabic. This is the main language in Algeria, and the French language is secondary. Listing 5-8 modifies the data and creates new rows for this second example. (Obviously, don't forget a commit statement if you're running in an Oracle database!)

Listing 5-8. Changing the Source Data

```
UPDATE Countries_Languages
SET Language_Category = 'SECONDARY'
WHERE Country_Id = 4 AND Language_Id = 2;
DELETE Countries_Languages
WHERE Country_Id = 6 AND Language_Id = 2;
INSERT INTO Countries_Languages (CL_Id, Country_Id, Language_Id,
Language_Category)
VALUES (14, 2, 2, 'SECONDARY');
INSERT INTO Languages (Language_Id, Language_Name)
VALUES (7, 'Algerian Arabic');
```

```
INSERT INTO Countries (Country_Id, Country_Code, Country_Name, Continent)
VALUES (10, 'Ag', 'Algeria', 'Africa');
INSERT INTO Countries_Languages (CL_Id, Country_Id, Language_Id,
Language_Category)
VALUES (15, 10, 7, 'MAIN');
INSERT INTO Countries_Languages (CL_Id, Country_Id, Language_Id,
Language_Category)
VALUES (16, 10, 3, 'SECONDARY');
```

Obviously, things are more complicated now! You are not simply deleting the target table anymore, either the English or French reporting table. You are also trying to keep the reporting tables syncronized with the source tables and applying the changes that have been made to the sources.

More than that, you need to be able to syncronize deletions. Whenever you delete a country from the sources, you need to remove it from the reporting table. When you have a new country in the source, you need to add it in the target, and when you change something in the source, you need to update the information in the target. This is the incremental data transfer.

Note that the business key is apart from the primary key in the source table, Countries_Languages. The business key is composed of the columns Country_Code and Language_Category. The role of the artificial key is just for unique identification and the role of the unique business key is to be sure that any unique row has relevance from the business point of view.

One country may have one category at a time. This one is subject to change, as in the Malta case. Based on the language category, you can detect the changes using either the atomic approach or the holistic approach. You can check for the differences one by one using the atomic approach, or you can check for the differences for all the countries using the holistic approach.

The Atomic Approach

You will solve this exercise by deleting the non-synchronized values and adding the list of new values. You can try to do so by thinking atomically and defining two cursors: one for the deletions of English countries that were changed in the source that will be applied first and the second one for the new values. You can see this atomic approach in Listing 5-9 (Oracle) and Listing 5-10 (SQL Server).

Listing 5-9. Incremental Data Transfer, Atomic Style, in Oracle

```
CREATE PROCEDURE Atomic_Inc_Transfer_English
AS
    v_Country_Name VARCHAR (50);
    v_Country_Code VARCHAR (3);
    v_Language_Category VARCHAR (10);
    v_Next_EEC_Id  INT;
    v_Count INT;
```

71

```
    CURSOR c_Existing_Countries IS
    SELECT Country_Code, Language_Category
    FROM English_European_Countries;

    CURSOR c_New_Countries IS
    SELECT c.Country_Name, c.Country_Code, cl.Language_Category
    FROM Countries_Languages cl INNER JOIN Languages l
        ON (l.Language_Id = cl.Language_Id)
    INNER JOIN Countries c ON (c.Country_Id = cl.Country_Id)
    WHERE l.Language_Name = 'English';
BEGIN
    OPEN c_Existing_Countries;

    LOOP
        FETCH c_Existing_Countries INTO v_Country_Code, v_Language_Category;

        EXIT WHEN c_Existing_Countries%NOTFOUND;

        SELECT COUNT(1) INTO v_Count
        FROM Countries_Languages cl INNER JOIN Languages l
            ON (l.Language_Id = cl.Language_Id)
        INNER JOIN Countries c ON (c.Country_Id = cl.Country_Id)
        WHERE l.Language_Name = 'English'
        AND c.Country_Code = v_Country_Code AND cl.Language_Category =
        v_Language_Category;

        IF (v_Count = 0) THEN
            DELETE English_European_Countries
            WHERE Country_Code = v_Country_Code AND Language_Category =
            v_Language_Category;
        END IF;

        COMMIT;
    END LOOP;

    CLOSE c_Existing_Countries;

    OPEN c_New_Countries;

    LOOP
        FETCH c_New_Countries INTO v_Country_Name, v_Country_Code,
        v_Language_Category;

        EXIT WHEN c_New_Countries%NOTFOUND;
```

```
    SELECT COUNT(*) INTO v_Count FROM dual
    WHERE NOT EXISTS
    (
        SELECT 1
        FROM English_European_Countries eec1
        WHERE eec1.Country_Code = v_Country_Code
        AND eec1.Language_Category = v_Language_Category
    );

    IF (v_Count = 1) THEN
        SELECT MAX (English_CL_Id) + 1 INTO v_Next_EEC_Id FROM
        English_European_Countries;

        INSERT INTO English_European_Countries (English_CL_Id,
        Country_Code, Country_Name, Language_Category)
        VALUES (v_Next_EEC_Id, v_Country_Code, v_Country_Name,
        v_Language_Category);
    END IF;

    COMMIT;

  END LOOP;

CLOSE c_New_Countries;
END Atomic_Inc_Transfer_English;
/
```

The logic in this example looks so professional! Let's analyze it.

1. You declare two cursors, one for storing the countries that should be deleted and another for storing the list of new countries.

2. You use the unique business key composed of Country_Code and Language_Category, and store the pair in two variables, row by row. The values are taken from the target table, English_European_Countries.

3. You check in the source system country by country, and filter per the combination country code and language category, for the English language. You calculate the count and add it in a dedicated variable.

4. If the count is zero, the data does not exist in the source system anymore, so it should be deleted from the target system.

5. Secondly, you open the second cursor from the source system.

6. You store the required information in the dedicated variables: country name, code, and the category of the language.

7. You check in the reporting table against the sources to see if you have new countries. You rely on the business key, of course. You calculate another count to see if you have something.

8. If the respective count is one, you consider the country as new and add it to the reporting table.

This task could have been accomplished in different ways in the atomic approach; this is just one solution to the problem. The important aspect here is to see the atomic approach in action: everything is imagined per unit and row by row.

Now let's see the SQL Server version of the atomic approach; it's very similar to the Oracle version, but there are differences due to the different nature of the programming language, which is another disadvantage of the atomic approach.

Using the atomic approach, which generally means using procedural code, requires a better understanding of the procedural language. The logic may be completely different when using the atomic approach because the programming languages are distinct, despite similarities.

Check the reporting table with English countries before and after the execution to see how the reporting table is synchronized with the sources. Do this for both the atomic approach now and the holistic approach later. Remember to start at the same initial conditions if you want to be 100% accurate.

Listing 5-10. Incremental Data Transfer, Atomic Style, in SQL Server

```
CREATE PROCEDURE Atomic_Inc_Transfer_English
AS
    DECLARE @v_Country_Name VARCHAR (50);
    DECLARE @v_Country_Code VARCHAR (3);
    DECLARE @v_Language_Category VARCHAR (10);
    DECLARE @v_Next_EEC_Id INT;
    DECLARE @v_Count INT;

    DECLARE c_Existing_Countries CURSOR FOR
    SELECT Country_Code, Language_Category
    FROM English_European_Countries;

    DECLARE c_Get_New_Countries CURSOR FOR
    SELECT c.Country_Name, c.Country_Code, cl.Language_Category
    FROM Countries_Languages cl INNER JOIN Languages l
        ON (l.Language_Id = cl.Language_Id)
    INNER JOIN Countries c ON (c.Country_Id = cl.Country_Id)
    WHERE l.Language_Name = 'English';
```

```
BEGIN
    OPEN c_Existing_Countries;

    FETCH NEXT FROM c_Existing_Countries INTO @v_Country_Code,
    @v_Language_Category;

WHILE (@@FETCH_STATUS = 0)
BEGIN
SET @v_Count = (SELECT COUNT (1)
FROM Countries_Languages cl INNER JOIN Languages l
    ON (l.Language_Id = cl.Language_Id)
INNER JOIN Countries c ON (c.Country_Id = cl.Country_Id)
WHERE l.Language_Name = 'English'
AND c.Country_Code = @v_Country_Code AND cl.Language_Category = @v_Language_
Category
            );
IF (@v_Count = 0)
BEGIN
    DELETE English_European_Countries
    WHERE Country_Code = @v_Country_Code AND Language_Category =
@v_Language_Category;
END;

FETCH NEXT FROM c_Existing_Countries INTO @v_Country_Code, @v_Language_
Category;
END

 CLOSE c_Existing_Countries;

 DEALLOCATE c_Existing_Countries;

 OPEN c_Get_New_Countries

 FETCH NEXT FROM c_Get_New_Countries INTO @v_Country_Name, @v_Country_Code,
@v_Language_Category;

 WHILE (@@FETCH_STATUS = 0)
 BEGIN

        SELECT @v_Count = COUNT(*)
        WHERE NOT EXISTS
        (
            SELECT 1
            FROM English_European_Countries eec1
            WHERE eec1.Country_Code = @v_Country_Code
            AND eec1.Language_Category = @v_Language_Category
        );
```

```
IF (@v_Count = 1)
BEGIN
    SET @v_Next_EEC_Id = (SELECT MAX (English_CL_Id) + 1 FROM English_
    European_Countries);

    INSERT INTO English_European_Countries (English_CL_Id, Country_Code,
    Country_Name, Language_Category)
    VALUES (@v_Next_EEC_Id, @v_Country_Code, @v_Country_Name, @v_
    Language_Category);
END;

FETCH NEXT FROM c_Get_New_Countries INTO @v_Country_Name, @v_Country_Code,
@v_Language_Category;
END

CLOSE c_Get_New_Countries;

DEALLOCATE c_Get_New_Countries;
END;
GO
```

Execute the procedures and check the reporting tables. See how Malta is a secondary language now, how Switzerland was deleted from the reporting table, and how Austria was added. Check all of this in the English_European_Countries table, comparing the results before and after the execution.

Comparing the two stored procedures, the Oracle and SQL Server versions, you can see almost the same steps. The while is a loop, the cursor is a cursor, the variable is a variable with or without the @ sign, the fetch is a fetch, the if statement is the same statement. In the end, it is not difficult to write in one system or another; things are similar. Portability is not the main problem; the performance and the clarity of the code are the problems.

The Holistic Solution

The holistic approach is much simpler. It's given in Listing 5-11 for SQL Server and in Listing 5-12 for Oracle. You don't need anything like cursors or variables in the holistic approach. All you need is to think holistically and understand that you have a set of data to affect with two actions.

Listing 5-11. Incremental Data Transfer, Holistic Style, in SQL Server

```
CREATE PROCEDURE Holistic_Inc_Transfer_English
AS
BEGIN
    DELETE FROM English_European_Countries
    FROM English_European_Countries eec
    WHERE NOT EXISTS
```

```
(
    SELECT 1
    FROM Countries_Languages cl INNER JOIN Languages l ON
    (l.Language_Id = cl.Language_Id)
    INNER JOIN Countries c ON (c.Country_Id = cl.Country_Id)
    WHERE l.Language_Name = 'English'
    AND eec.Country_Code = c.Country_Code
    AND eec.Language_Category = cl.Language_Category
);

INSERT INTO English_European_Countries (English_CL_Id, Country_Code,
Country_Name, Language_Category)
SELECT (SELECT MAX (English_CL_Id) AS Max_English_CL_Id FROM English_
European_Countries) + ROW_NUMBER() OVER (ORDER BY c.Country_Code,
cl.Language_Category) AS English_CL_Id, c.Country_Code,
c.Country_Name, cl.Language_Category
FROM Countries_Languages cl INNER JOIN Languages l ON (l.Language_Id =
cl.Language_Id)
INNER JOIN Countries c ON (c.Country_Id = cl.Country_Id)
WHERE l.Language_Name = 'English'
AND NOT EXISTS
(
    SELECT 1 FROM English_European_Countries eec
    WHERE eec.Language_Category = cl.Language_Category AND eec.Country_
    Code = c.Country_Code
);
END;
GO
```

Let's see the steps.

1. First, you delete the countries from the reporting table that don't conform to the business key and were eliminated from the set of source tables. You have all the items that need to be removed in a single select statement. You identify the rows to be removed in a simple select statement and then transform this into a delete statement.

2. Second, you add the new English European countries that do not exist in the reporting target table. You generate an artificial key for the reporting key in the select statement using different SQL features.

Now let's compare the two approaches. You have one delete statement and one insert statement; that's it! You might need to check a select statement to identify the data that needs to be deleted.

Let's assume you tested the data before. You look at the data and try to understand the nature. You look to see if what you have is indeed what needs to be deleted and, afterwards, you transform this select statement into a delete statement.

You think in these terms. There are some countries in the reporting table that may be obsolete due to some changes in the source tables. Let's see these countries first. You have a set of countries, one single data set. There's no reason to go country by country; there's a list of countries, a set of rows, and you want to identify this list. This list, once correctly identified, can be used for the deletion. In the logic, there is one delete statement. In reality, we always think of the delete action in three steps: we have a set of rows, we identify it, and we change it into a delete.

Secondly, and similarly, you have another set of countries that needs to be added in the reporting table. You take the select statement and make sure to identify the correct set of new countries. You find a way to dynamically generate new artificial identifiers for the key in the reporting table. There's no reason to move the logic at the atomic level.

Let's analyze the Oracle logic in the holistic approach and compare it to the SQL Server logic. You will be amazed to see how similar the logic is. Actually, if you weren't inside a stored procedure and you executed everything in a SQL editor, you could copy the entire piece of code from Oracle and execute it in SQL Server or vice versa.

Listing 5-12. Incremental Data Transfer, Holistic Style, in Oracle

```
CREATE PROCEDURE Holistic_Inc_Transfer_English
AS
BEGIN
DELETE FROM English_European_Countries eec
WHERE NOT EXISTS
(
    SELECT 1
    FROM Countries_Languages cl INNER JOIN Languages l
        ON (l.Language_Id = cl.Language_Id)
    INNER JOIN Countries c
        ON (c.Country_Id = cl.Country_Id)
    WHERE l.Language_Name = 'English'
    AND eec.Country_Code = c.Country_Code
    AND eec.Language_Category = cl.Language_Category
);

INSERT INTO English_European_Countries (English_CL_Id, Country_Code,
Country_Name, Language_Category)
SELECT (SELECT MAX (English_CL_Id) AS Max_English_CL_Id
FROM English_European_Countries) + ROW_NUMBER() OVER (ORDER BY c.Country_
Code, cl.Language_Category) AS English_CL_Id, c.Country_Code,
c.Country_Name, cl.Language_Category
FROM Countries_Languages cl INNER JOIN Languages l
    ON (l.Language_Id = cl.Language_Id)
INNER JOIN Countries c
    ON (c.Country_Id = cl.Country_Id)
WHERE l.Language_Name = 'English'
```

```
AND NOT EXISTS
(
    SELECT 1 FROM English_European_Countries eec
    WHERE eec.Language_Category = cl.Language_Category
    AND eec.Country_Code = c.Country_Code
);
END Holistic_Inc_Transfer_English;
/
```

You just analyzed two simple examples of data transfer. The data transfer, which is a copy process from a source to a destination, is the most common task for a programmer when writing inside the database. In these examples, you first transferred the data in a simple full approach: the data was completely deleted first and replaced with the data from the sources. The second exercise increased the complexity: the data in the target was not deleted first. The data was incrementally updated, and only the changes were applied to the target. In both scenarios, the artificial identifier in the target needed to be dynamically generated.

This data transfer problem can be solved in both ways, according to the two visions and styles of development. The application developers will be tempted to open cursors and to move the context and the transfer to the row level. Because they are not fully aware of the fact that they are in a relational database, where the data is affected in data sets, and they know just the principles of structure programming, they imagine that they can transfer everything at the row level.

By contrast, the database developers or the flexible application developers famdliarized with the set based approach are aware of the data set. They know that the data should be handled in data sets, and they always try to identify and affect the data set as a whole, in a holistic manner. They know that there are many set-based facilities in every database system for various things. For example, they use the row number function to generate the identifier, and this function is applied per the entire data set. Their logic is much simpler, more condensed, set-oriented, more performant, and portable because SQL is a standard, so the logic is almost the same in any database system. The transfer occurs at the level of the entire data set. This requires a certain style of development, one that is different from the style of the user interface. It may not be attractive to some programmers, but it is efficient and it is what it should be used in a relational database.

■ ■ ■

CHAPTER 6

The Challenge of Scalar Functions

The cursor is the main feature that allows the application developer to move the entire context to the row level. From my point of view, when teaching application developers to work in the database, I would completely remove the cursor from their work agenda and forbid the use of it until they learn and **understand the concept of the data set**. I would also remove the loop feature from their development activity and not allow them to loop under any circumstances. Cursors with loops are the favorite tools of many application programmers, who like to use them often because they handle things atomically.

The truth is that the cursor is a great feature and it allows us to solve many problems in the atomic style when the holistic style is not satisfactory. There are many situations when we need them and when the data set cannot be handled as a whole so we are forced to move the context from data set to the row level. So please don't believe that I reject cursors on the whole. On the contrary, I believe that the cursor is a great feature by itself; the abuse of cursors is a disaster.

Cursors Have Their Place

To be honest, I like working with cursors! The steps are very clear. Declaring the cursor, opening it, moving intermediate columns or expressions from the cursor data set into the layer of variables, moving through the loop from one row to another, and performing various manipulations are all challenging and exciting actions.

Many programming ideas can only be understood and clarified in time. Even now, I continue to discover new things and clarify others. For example, cursors and their mechanisms are fascinating. Especially when trees are involved, it's difficult to handle the logic; this is when we need to use cursors. The use of cursors is a perfect feature for the atomic approach. It allows us to change the context from the data set to data row. Sometimes this switch is required.

The atomic approach itself is mandatory and critical, and we cannot live without it. However, the atomic approach should be seen as a **backup** solution for the holistic approach within a relational database. This is a crucial point. It is similar to the use of antibiotics; no one can say that antibiotics are bad. They add many years to the average lifespan. However, excessive use of antibiotics is a bad practice, and doctors recommend avoiding using

S. Ardeleanu, *Relational Database Programming*, DOI 10.1007/978-1-4842-2080-1_6

antibiotics unless they are necessary. The same way that the excessive use of antibiotics will damage the body in time, the use of the atomic approach will damage a database in time.

The Lure of Functions

The application developer is a great fan of the cursor for another reason. As we all know, one of the most important features for an application developer is the function. The application developers loves functions and they like to use them as much as they can. In specific programming languages like PL SQL or Transact SQL, these functions are named **scalar functions**.

A scalar function returns a certain value of a certain type, like a string or number. The scalar functions are very suitable for the atomic approach because they can be applied per variables within loops and cursors. As with stored procedures, if the application developer sees a stored procedure like a scalar function returning a void, they know that a stored procedure should be defined to act in one expression or value and this action can be executed atomically within a loop in a cursor.

So what are the connections between the cursor, the scalar function, and the atomic approach? The cursor and the loop allow you to go down from the data set to the data row. The scalar function accepts variables as parameters, it returns discrete values, and it is a type of function that is executed per row. The scalar function is a row function; it is exactly what the application developer needs to be able to move the context of development from the data set to the data row. When I say to move the context from the data set to the data row, I don't mean that the application developers are necessarily aware of the context switch. In most cases, they are not aware of any data set and they go down to the row level by instinct, automatically.

The principle of structured programming teaches us to create functions and to use them to divide the logic into smaller pieces. One of the first things the students learn is the use of functions. They learn to create functions, they learn that the function will return something in most cases, and they learn to add parameters to the functions and recall them later in their logic. When they start to work in the database and see the scalar functions, they make the connection right away to what they already know from classic programming.

Of course, those functions are useful in the database too. But not all functions are scalar, per row. There are set-based functions like table functions, for example. There are alternatives in almost any database programming language. The function can be applied to a data set and it can return a data set. The function can be used holistically. Unfortunately, nothing compares to scalar functions for application developers because they remind them of what they know from the user interface. They are tempted to use scalar functions in excess; they combine them with cursors and loops, and they imposes the atomic style in the database.

Divide and Conquer

One of the most important principles in structured programming is to divide complex problems into simpler ones by using functions or procedures. This is a great principle and it is followed in database programming too. But that doesn't mean to divide the problem at the data row level instead of trying to solve it at the data set level. Solving problems at the data set level, which is how it should be in database programming, may generate a smaller number of routines as a secondary consequence. However, this is no tragedy. This principle is not valuable by itself but for the benefits it brings to the software application. We are not dealing with ethics, metaphysics, or even a science like geometry where principles should be respected under any circumstances and regardless of any consequences. We are in the practical world of software development and we are in the database. The use of functions is different here than in the user interface, and the holistic approach generally means less and different routines, especially in specific systems like a data migration interface between system A and system B.

If you look at the types of available functions, you can see that every database programming language has many types of functions. In SQL Server, there are table functions, which return a set of values in the form of an object called a table variable. Similarly, there is the possibility of returning complex types in PL SQL like arrays or collections. This shows that all database engines and their associated programming languages offer the option to use functions in a holistic approach. Some of these functions may be required and may be used. Very often, though, the use of functions causes bad performance and so should be avoided.

Scalar functions in particular are part of a serious performance issue if applied to large data sets inside cursors. Let's imagine one set of values with thousands of rows. You can create a function and call that function in a cursor thousands of times. Or you can manipulate the entire data set using some simple SQL statements. These kinds of applications should be set-oriented but are row-oriented. One of the rules I would state in these kinds of applications is this one: use scalar functions for system settings if you want to identify one setting or another in some configuration tables. Do not use scalar functions for operations that involve data sets. Solve the problem at the level of the data set.

Identify the level of granularity required by your software application. If it's a set-oriented application, forget about scalar functions. Most of the time they won't be used because these functions apply to details and require the atomic level.

So when should you use scalar functions? There is one situation when scalar functions are excellent in the database. Let's define the concept of scalar query, by analogy with a scalar function. A scalar query is that type of query that returns one single value of a certain type, like a string value or numeric one. Very often, configuration tables are suitable for scalar queries if they read from the configuration tables. The scalar queries are ideal for scalar functions and are excellent especially for configurations tables, so they may be used intensively in the database.

Example 3: Filtered Full Data Transfer

This next example is a more complex scenario that builds on Example 1 from Chapter 5. This new example is a full data transfer between two systems. The same design applies but the conditions for the report table generation are not so simple anymore. The data transfer will be filtered and some conditions will occur based on whether the transfer will take place.

The business (technical) request is as follows: you need to generate the same report table, in the full approach used in Chapter 5, with one difference. The data should be generated from the set of three source tables into the target-reporting table, either English or French, under certain conditions. If the language is the principal language (or MAIN), you need to check for the flag. If the flag is set to a positive value like 1, then you will generate the English or French set of countries into the table.

Note that the business (technical) description is clearly written in the atomic style. The problem has been defined atomically before any line of code was written anywhere!

The application developer will follow his dear, classic, structured philosophy, completely atomic and procedural. Our dear Joanna Doe likes functions so she will build some nice and cozy functions, scalar of course.

Our solutions are always driven by the business. The distinction between a business analyst and a software programmer is not always clearly made and very often programmers are also analysts. The first thing when doing any development is to make sure you know what you have to do.

On the other hand, the business request itself, explained by a developer, is clearly influenced by a developer experienced in writing code. If an application developer like Joanna sees things atomically, she will come up with reasons to write her specs atomically. She can easily blame the business later, saying that she was instructed to write the code in a certain way due to the way the business request was written!

The Atomic Solutions

The application developer will see things per the business key, the combination between language and country. If you look at the design of the table, you can see that the business key is composed of a language and a country corresponding to the unique constraint named UQ_Language_Country. This is the key to the atomic approach because the application developer knows that they can have one set of attributes or characteristics per country and language. Therefore, the functions will be oriented per language and country, and these fields will be the parameters for the scalar functions.

Listing 6-1 shows the two functions in the SQL Server solution. The first function returns the category of the language for the respective country. The category can be either principal (MAIN) or secondary (SECONDARY). This function is a get function, of course, and the function is get_category. The second function returns the flag (make_flag) for the same combination of language and country; the function is named get_flag. Let's see the nice scalar functions!

Listing 6-1. Scalar Functions, Atomic Style, in SQL Server

```
CREATE FUNCTION get_category
(
    @p_language_id INT,
    @p_country_id INT
)
RETURNS VARCHAR(10)
BEGIN
    DECLARE @v_category VARCHAR(10);
    DECLARE @v_count INT;

    SELECT @v_count = COUNT(*) FROM countries_languages
    WHERE language_id = @p_language_id AND country_id = @p_country_id;
```

```
    IF @v_count = 0
        SET @v_category = NULL
    ELSE
        SELECT @v_category = Language_Category FROM countries_languages
        WHERE language_id = @p_language_id AND country_id = @p_country_id;

    RETURN @v_category;
END
GO
CREATE FUNCTION get_flag
(
    @p_language_id INT,
    @p_country_id INT
)
RETURNS INT
BEGIN
    DECLARE @v_make_flag INT
    DECLARE @v_count     INT

    SELECT @v_count = COUNT(*) FROM countries_languages
    WHERE language_id = @p_language_id AND country_id = @p_country_id;

    IF @v_count = 0
        SET @v_make_flag = NULL
    ELSE
        SELECT @v_make_flag = Make_Flag FROM countries_languages
        WHERE language_id = @p_language_id AND country_id = @p_country_id;

    RETURN @v_make_flag;
END
GO
```

These functions specify, for each language and country, the value for the flag and category, MAIN or SECONDARY. These functions allow the developer to identify the conditions specified in the business requirement. The assumption when building these functions is clearly atomic and procedural; the programmer already sees one country and one language. **He sees himself as a rider on the row! Unfortunately, the row is not a horse but a donkey!**

- Looking at the scalar functions in Listing 6-1, you can describe them very easily in accordance with the business description.

- You assume from the beginning that you are positioned in one language and one country. You can see this by looking at the parameters of the functions: language and country. From the beginning you see that you can think atomically because you consider yourself as being inline with one country and one language.

85

- Looking at the name of the function and the return type, you see that the function is scalar and you understand that the function will return a certain category, which is a field of type string. For the second function you see that the return type is an integer and you understand that you will receive the flag.

- Per every country and language, you check a count to see if you have anything for that language and country in the association table (countries_languages). If not, you set the return value to null.

- If you have anything in the association table, you will get the category or the flag in a dedicated variable and you can specify that variable as the return value for the function.

You can see the atomic vision even before the function is called. The house for the scalar functions will be the cursor, of course.

Now, when the developer is ready for the final call, he will use a similar logic to the one in Chapter 5, but now it will be even better because she can use her dear scalar functions and call them in the cursor, so the database will be the mirror of what she knows from her classic development. Look at Listing 6-2 and see the atomic style for SQL Server.

Listing 6-2. Full Filtered Data Transfer, Atomic Style, in SQL Server

```
CREATE PROCEDURE Atomic_Transfer_Country_Flag
(
  @p_Language_Name VARCHAR (50)
)
AS
        DECLARE @v_Country_Name VARCHAR (50),
@v_Country_Code VARCHAR (3);
        DECLARE @v_Language_Category VARCHAR (10),
@v_New_EEC_Id INT;
        DECLARE @v_Country_Id INT, @v_Language_Id INT,
@v_Make_Flag INT;
        DECLARE c_Get_Countries_Lang CURSOR FOR
        SELECT Country_Id, Language_Id
        FROM Countries_Languages
        WHERE Language_Id IN (SELECT Language_Id FROM Languages WHERE
        Language_Name = @p_Language_Name);
BEGIN
        SET @v_New_EEC_Id = 1;
        IF @p_Language_Name = 'English'
                DELETE English_European_Countries;
        ELSE IF @p_Language_Name = 'French'
                DELETE French_European_Countries;
        OPEN c_Get_Countries_Lang
        FETCH NEXT FROM c_Get_Countries_Lang
        INTO @v_Country_Id, @v_Language_Id;
```

```
WHILE (@@FETCH_STATUS = 0)
BEGIN
        SET @v_Language_Category = dbo.get_category(@v_Language_Id,
        @v_Country_Id);
        IF @v_Language_Category = 'MAIN'
        BEGIN
                SET @v_Make_Flag = dbo.get_flag (@v_Language_Id,
                @v_Country_Id);
                IF @v_Make_Flag = 1
                BEGIN
                        SELECT @v_Country_Name = Country_Name, @v_
                        Country_Code = Country_Code FROM countries
                        WHERE Country_Id = @v_Country_Id;
                        IF @p_Language_Name = 'English'
                                INSERT INTO English_European_
                                Countries (English_CL_Id, Country_
                                Code, Country_Name, Language_
                                Category)
                                VALUES (@v_New_EEC_Id, @v_Country_
                                Code, @v_Country_Name, @v_Language_
                                Category);
                        ELSE IF @p_Language_Name = 'French'
                                INSERT INTO French_European_
                                Countries (French_CL_Id, Country_
                                Code, Country_Name, Language_
                                Category)
                                VALUES (@v_New_EEC_Id, @v_Country_
                                Code, @v_Country_Name, @v_Language_
                                Category);
                        SET @v_New_EEC_Id = @v_New_EEC_Id + 1;
                END
        END
        FETCH NEXT FROM c_Get_Countries_Lang INTO @v_Country_Id,
        @v_Language_Id;
END
CLOSE c_Get_Countries_Lang;
DEALLOCATE c_Get_Countries_Lang;
END;
GO
```

Let's analyze this logic, written in a very classic style and in full compliance with the business description of the problem. The business analyst that described the problem was already under the influence of the atomic approach. This is not an excuse for the developers because they can use their own mind and they can correctly interpret the statements.

The steps are the following:

1. Declare the cursor with all the combinations of language and country. Open it. Fetch the identifiers for both country and language. These will be used as parameters for the scalar functions.

2. Initialize the value for the artificial identifier.

3. Delete the reporting table, either English or French.

4. Calculate the category for the language and country, using the function get_category. The parameters are taken from the variables generated from the cursor.

5. If the category is MAIN, continue the logic in the most pure procedural style and calculate the flag using the second function, get_flag.

6. If the flag is positive (value 1), generate the data in the reporting table.

7. You can see the results after executing Malta and New Zealand for English European countries and Canada for French European countries.

Let's see the logic in Oracle, and start with the functions. Listing 6-3 shows the Oracle versions of the two functions from Listing 6-1. As you can see, things are similar; the procedural syntax differs but not so much that it's difficult to translate the functions from one database brand to the other.

Listing 6-3. Scalar Functions, Atomic Style, in Oracle

```
CREATE OR REPLACE FUNCTION get_category
(
    p_language_id INT,
    p_country_id INT
)
RETURN VARCHAR2
AS
    v_category VARCHAR2(10);
    v_count INT;
BEGIN
    SELECT COUNT(*) INTO v_count FROM countries_languages
    WHERE language_id = p_language_id AND country_id = p_country_id;

    IF v_count = 0 THEN
        v_category := NULL;
    ELSE
        SELECT Language_Category INTO v_category FROM countries_languages
        WHERE language_id = p_language_id AND country_id = p_country_id;
    END IF;
```

```
        RETURN v_category;
END;
/
CREATE FUNCTION get_flag
(
    p_language_id INT,
    p_country_id INT
)
RETURN  INT
AS
    v_make_flag INT;
    v_count INT;
BEGIN
    SELECT COUNT(*) INTO v_count FROM countries_languages
    WHERE language_id = p_language_id AND country_id = p_country_id;

    IF v_count = 0 THEN
        v_make_flag := NULL;
    ELSE
        SELECT Make_Flag INTO v_make_flag FROM countries_languages
        WHERE language_id = p_language_id AND country_id = p_country_id;
    END IF;

    RETURN v_make_flag;
END;
/
```

You may see a similar style in any system. The programmer uses the same atomic style, the same mind, and the same confusions; old habits can't be changed, despite the necessities. Hello, my dear developers: wake up! We are in the database, we are in a relational database, and it is a different world. Listing 6-4 shows how the Oracle or PL/SQL developer ends his logic in triumph!

Listing 6-4. Full Filtered Data Transfer, Atomic Style, in Oracle

```
CREATE OR REPLACE PROCEDURE Atomic_Transfer_Country_Flag
(
 p_Language_Name VARCHAR
)
AS
  v_Country_Name VARCHAR (50);
  v_Country_Code VARCHAR (3);
  v_Language_Category VARCHAR (10);
  v_New_EEC_Id INT;
  v_Country_Id INT;
  v_Language_Id INT;
  v_Make_Flag INT;
  CURSOR c_Get_Countries_Lang IS
 SELECT Country_Id, Language_Id
```

```
 FROM Countries_Languages
 WHERE Language_Id IN (SELECT Language_Id FROM Languages
WHERE Language_Name = p_Language_Name);
BEGIN
        v_New_EEC_Id := 1;
        IF p_Language_Name = 'English' THEN
                DELETE English_European_Countries;
        ELSIF p_Language_Name = 'French' THEN
                French_European_Countries;
        END IF;
        OPEN c_Get_Countries_Lang;
        LOOP
                FETCH c_Get_Countries_Lang
INTO v_Country_Id, v_Language_Id;
                EXIT WHEN c_Get_Countries_Lang%NOTFOUND;
                        v_Language_Category := get_category(v_Language_Id,
                        v_Country_Id);
                        IF v_Language_Category = 'MAIN' THEN
                v_Make_Flag := get_flag (v_Language_Id, v_Country_Id);
                                IF v_Make_Flag = 1 THEN
                                SELECT Country_Name, Country_Code INTO
                                v_Country_Name, v_Country_Code
                        FROM countries WHERE Country_Id = v_Country_Id;
                                        IF p_Language_Name = 'English' THEN
                                                INSERT INTO English_
                                                European_Countries (English_
                                                CL_Id, Country_Code, Country_
                                                Name, Language_Category)
                                        VALUES (v_New_EEC_Id, v_Country_
                                        Code, v_Country_Name, v_Language_
                                        Category);
                                        ELSIF p_Language_Name = 'French' THEN
                                                INSERT INTO French_European_
                                                Countries (French_CL_Id,
                                                Country_Code, Country_Name,
                                                Language_Category)
                                                VALUES (v_New_EEC_Id,
                                                v_Country_Code, v_Country_
                                                Name, v_Language_Category);
                                        END IF;
                                        v_New_EEC_Id := v_New_EEC_Id + 1;
                                END IF;
                        END IF;
                COMMIT;
        END LOOP;
 CLOSE c_Get_Countries_Lang;
END;
/
```

As you can see, this is a very impressive logical and procedural design, according to the business definition. The principles of structured programming are satisfied and the application developer is extremely happy. It does not matter that this code does not mean good performance for the database, that the number of lines of code is triple, and that the logic is infinitely more complex.

Regarding the results, if you check the reporting table, you can see that the UK is the only country that satisfies the business requirements.

The Holistic Solutions

Let's go back to the example and let's prepare the holistic solution for the exercise. Now you will see that even the business definition can be changed to be SQL oriented. What do you think about that? Any programmer, before doing any development work, should gather the requirements. Many programmers prepare their own requirements; few of them are lucky enough to work with specialized business analysts. Therefore, the first phase, the requirements, is very often done by the programmers. Even here, in this early stage, the vision can be atomic or holistic. Let's see the same business requirement from earlier in the chapter written in a total different style.

The business (technical) request: you need to generate the same report table in the full approach, as in Chapter 5, but with one difference. The data should be generated from the set of three source tables into the target reporting table, either English or French, for the countries where the language is principal (MAIN) and for the countries with the positive flag (1).

Now the text looks like a simple query, don't you think? This is exactly what it is. You need to generate the English or French European countries for the ones with the flag set to 1 and category of MAIN. It is a simple insert select statement, and the difference in the logic is obvious. Listing 6-5 shows the holistic approach for Oracle.

Listing 6-5. Full Filtered Data Transfer, Holistic Style, in Oracle

```
CREATE OR REPLACE PROCEDURE Holistic_Transfer_Country_Flag
(
  p_Language_Name VARCHAR
)
AS
BEGIN
        DELETE English_European_Countries
WHERE p_Language_Name = 'English';
        DELETE French_European_Countries
WHERE p_Language_Name = 'French';
    INSERT INTO English_European_Countries (English_CL_Id, Country_Code,
    Country_Name, Language_Category)
        SELECT ROW_NUMBER() OVER (ORDER BY c.Country_Code, cl.Language_
        Category) AS English_CL_Id, c.Country_Code,
        c.Country_Name, cl.Language_Category
        FROM Countries_Languages cl INNER JOIN Languages l
```

```
  ON (l.Language_Id = cl.Language_Id)
        INNER JOIN Countries c ON (c.Country_Id = cl.Country_Id)
        WHERE l.Language_Name = p_Language_Name AND p_Language_Name =
        'English' AND cl.Language_Category = 'MAIN' AND cl.Make_Flag = 1;
    INSERT INTO French_European_Countries (French_CL_Id, Country_Code,
    Country_Name, Language_Category)
        SELECT ROW_NUMBER() OVER (ORDER BY c.Country_Code, cl.Language_
        Category) AS French_CL_Id, c.Country_Code,
        c.Country_Name, cl.Language_Category
        FROM Countries_Languages cl INNER JOIN Languages l
ON (l.Language_Id = cl.Language_Id)
        INNER JOIN Countries c ON (c.Country_Id = cl.Country_Id)
        WHERE l.Language_Name = p_Language_Name
AND p_Language_Name = 'French'
AND cl.Language_Category = 'MAIN' AND cl.Make_Flag = 1;
        COMMIT;
END Holistic_Transfer_Country_Flag;
/
```

This is the set-based approach and the holistic style of development, the one that is recommended in the relational database and that should be used by every programmer, not just by specialized database developers. Let's examine and compare the two logics and see the difference in style. In the holistic approach, there is no procedural logic at all, just pure SQL.

Let's see the steps.

1. The countries with the language specified as parameter are deleted. There is no if-else statement and the language specifies just the filter condition. I intentionally removed the if-else to show that the procedural code can be avoided and replaced with the use of SQL.

2. The countries are populated for English or French from the set of source tables. Similarly, the use of filter conditions after the language parameter replaces the if-else statement.

3. Just to clarify, one language will be transferred based on the value of the parameter. The other will not be affected at all because the filter condition for the language will not be satisfied. The reason for this approach was to show that the procedural code is very often optional. I also wanted to maximize the use of SQL and minimize the use of procedural code.

The data in the target is generated easily and straightforward, in a holistic manner. The data set, depending on the value of the parameter, is generated according to the language. The difference compared to Exercise 1 from Chapter 5 is that two new additional filter conditions were added to the logic. They replace the scalar functions and the rest of the additional procedural facilities. Regarding portability, see how the SQL server version in Listing 6-6 is almost the same as the Oracle solution from Listing 6-5. This similarity is one of the advantages of the holistic style.

Listing 6-6. Full Filtered Data Transfer, Holistic Style, in SQL Server

```
CREATE PROCEDURE Holistic_Transfer_Country_Flag
(
  @p_Language_Name VARCHAR (50)
)
AS
BEGIN
        DELETE English_European_Countries
WHERE @p_Language_Name = 'English';
        DELETE French_European_Countries
WHERE @p_Language_Name = 'French';
  INSERT INTO English_European_Countries (English_CL_Id, Country_Code,
  Country_Name, Language_Category)
        SELECT ROW_NUMBER() OVER (ORDER BY c.Country_Code, cl.Language_
        Category) AS English_CL_Id, c.Country_Code,
        c.Country_Name, cl.Language_Category
        FROM Countries_Languages cl INNER JOIN Languages l
  ON (l.Language_Id = cl.Language_Id)
        INNER JOIN Countries c ON (c.Country_Id = cl.Country_Id)
        WHERE l.Language_Name = @p_Language_Name
AND @p_Language_Name = 'English'
        AND cl.Language_Category = 'MAIN' AND cl.Make_Flag = 1;
    INSERT INTO French_European_Countries (French_CL_Id, Country_Code,
    Country_Name, Language_Category)
        SELECT ROW_NUMBER() OVER (ORDER BY c.Country_Code, cl.Language_
        Category) AS French_CL_Id, c.Country_Code,
        c.Country_Name, cl.Language_Category
        FROM Countries_Languages cl INNER JOIN Languages l
ON (l.Language_Id = cl.Language_Id)
        INNER JOIN Countries c ON (c.Country_Id = cl.Country_Id)
        WHERE l.Language_Name = @p_Language_Name
AND @p_Language_Name = 'French'
        AND cl.Language_Category = 'MAIN' AND cl.Make_Flag = 1;
END
GO
```

To conclude, imagine that the quantity of data is moderate to medium large and imagine an atomic style. This scenario is not exotic; unfortunately, this is really happening in many databases all over the world. The performance of scalar functions in cursors is very poor and normally they should be minimized (with the exception of true scalar functions, when applied to scalar data sets, returning exactly one row, like configuration data).

In my data migration interface I used two scalar functions. They are used to get the values for configuration data, which are highly static data and useful for the functionality of the data migration interface. In this case, because these configuration values actually drive the entire data migration/replication system, I used scalar functions because their meaning is the same in any classic system. Apart from that scenario, I never use them because I don't need them; they are inefficient and they require the intensive use of cursors.

Example 4: A Simple Query

Let's continue to illustrate the two development approaches within the database. Let's see the context of a query. I know how important these examples are for any developer, experienced or not. Words and concepts are good; words and programming code are even better!

New Example Set

Future examples in this book will be based on a simple design composed of two tables: one contains a list of products and one is a list of the types of products with the associated foreign key. Listing 6-7 shows the table design.

Listing 6-7. Products Design

```
CREATE TABLE Product_Types
(
 Product_Type_Id INT CONSTRAINT  Nn_Product_Type_Id NOT NULL,
 Product_Type_Code VARCHAR (5)
CONSTRAINT  Nn_Product_Type_Code NOT NULL,
 Name VARCHAR (255) CONSTRAINT  Nn_Product_Type_Name NOT NULL,
 CONSTRAINT  Pk_Product_Type_Id PRIMARY KEY (Product_Type_Id)
);

CREATE TABLE Products
(
 Product_Id INT CONSTRAINT  Nn_Product_Id NOT NULL,
 Name VARCHAR (30) CONSTRAINT  Nn_Product_Name NOT NULL,
 Product_Code VARCHAR (5)
CONSTRAINT  Nn_Product_Code NOT NULL,
 Product_Description VARCHAR (255),
 Make_Flag INT,
 Product_Type_Id INT,
 Default_Quantity INT,
 CONSTRAINT  Pk_Product_Id PRIMARY KEY (Product_Id),
 CONSTRAINT  Fk_Products_Product_Types
FOREIGN KEY (Product_Type_Id)
 REFERENCES Product_Types (Product_Type_Id)
);
```

The table named Products contains the following columns:

1. The column Product_Id is a unique and artificial product identifier, and this is the primary key as well.

2. The column Product_Name represents the name of the product.

3. The column Product_Code represents the code of the product.

4. The column `Product_Description` represents the description of the product.

5. The flag called `Make_Flag` can be either zero or one.

6. The type of the product is specified as a reference to the table with product types.

7. The default quantity for the product will be used later.

Tables require data. Listing 6-8 puts some example data into the two tables.

Listing 6-8. Insert Script to Populate Products

```
INSERT INTO Product_Types (Product_Type_Id, Product_Type_Code, Name)
VALUES (1, 'C1', 'Product type 01 description');
INSERT INTO Product_Types (Product_Type_Id, Product_Type_Code, Name)
VALUES (2, 'C2', 'Product type 02 description');
INSERT INTO Product_Types (Product_Type_Id, Product_Type_Code, Name)
VALUES (3, 'D3', 'Product type 03 description');
INSERT INTO Products (Product_Id, Name, Product_Code, Make_Flag, Product_
Type_Id, Default_Quantity)
VALUES (1, 'Product 01', 'A1', 0, 1, 10);
INSERT INTO Products (Product_Id, Name, Product_Code, Make_Flag, Product_
Type_Id, Default_Quantity)
VALUES (2, 'Product 02', 'A2', 1, 2, 20);
INSERT INTO Products (Product_Id, Name, Product_Code, Make_Flag, Product_
Type_Id, Default_Quantity)
VALUES (3, 'Product 03', 'A3', 0, 1, 5);
INSERT INTO Products (Product_Id, Name, Product_Code, Make_Flag, Product_
Type_Id, Default_Quantity)
VALUES (4, 'Product 04', 'A4', 1, 3, 1);
INSERT INTO Products (Product_Id, Name, Product_Code, Make_Flag, Product_
Type_Id, Default_Quantity)
VALUES (5, 'Product 05', 'A5', 0, 1, 9);
INSERT INTO Products (Product_Id, Name, Product_Code, Make_Flag, Product_
Type_Id, Default_Quantity)
VALUES (6, 'Product 06', 'A6', 0, 1, 20);
INSERT INTO Products (Product_Id, Name, Product_Code, Make_Flag, Product_
Type_Id, Default_Quantity)
VALUES (7, 'Product 07', 'A7', 0, 2, 15);
INSERT INTO Products (Product_Id, Name, Product_Code, Make_Flag, Product_
Type_Id, Default_Quantity)
VALUES (8, 'Product 08', 'A8', 1, 3, 6);
INSERT INTO Products (Product_Id, Name, Product_Code, Make_Flag, Product_
Type_Id, Default_Quantity)
VALUES (9, 'Product 09', 'A9', 1, 1, 8);
INSERT INTO Products (Product_Id, Name, Product_Code, Make_Flag, Product_
Type_Id, Default_Quantity)
VALUES (10, 'Product 10', 'A10', 1, 2, 8);
```

Tables 6-1 and 6-2 show the values for the products and their types. Table 6-1 shows the product type values, and Table 6-2 shows the product values.

Table 6-1. *Sample Product Types Values*

Product Type Id	Product Type Code	Name
1	C1	Product type 01 description
2	C2	Product type 02 description
3	D3	Product type 03 description

Table 6-2. *Sample Product Values*

Product Id	Name	Code	Description	Make Flag	Pr Type Id	Default Quantity
1	Product 01	A1	NULL	0	1	10
2	Product 02	A2	NULL	1	2	20
3	Product 03	A3	NULL	0	1	5
4	Product 04	A4	NULL	1	3	1
5	Product 05	A5	NULL	0	1	9
6	Product 06	A6	NULL	0	1	20
7	Product 07	A7	NULL	0	2	15
8	Product 08	A8	NULL	1	3	6
9	Product 09	A9	NULL	1	1	8
10	Product 10	A10	NULL	1	2	8

Business Requirement

Everything starts with the business requirements. Now you have a simple design with some familiar products and their types. Let's see what you want from this list of products. The following is the first business requirement: *you want to get a simple result set, a data set taken from the* Products *table. You want to select the product identifier, the name for each product, the name for the previous product, and the product code for the previous product if the flag is set to 1 (otherwise the current product code). The concept of previous product is based on the product identifier. For example, the previous product for product id 3 is product id 2, etc.*

This exercise seems very suitable for the atomic approach because it looks like you need to access the data row by row and gather the information for the previous rows. This is a complex example and the use of the atomic approach may be understandable. That does not mean it can't be avoided, but you need to have good eyes and a good SQL-oriented mind to be able to see the holistic approach. For the moment, let's focus on the atomic approach that seems so unavoidable.

The Atomic Solutions

Any experienced application developer will start dividing everything into small pieces of code and will start imagining how to move the previous values into variables for each row, etc. You're working with 10 products, so it's not hard to work atomically from a performance point of view. However, this is actually a sample from a large table with thousands of products. If you need to dig into larger data sets atomically from the beginning, you should question whether there's another way to solve the problem!

Most developers are familiar with the atomic style because it is the one used at the user interface level. Thinking SQL and thinking holistically requires a different vision and a different style. The good news is that this style is simpler and it offers better performance. The differences in performance between the two styles when dealing with a significant quantity and variety of data are impressive for anyone who wants to do some testing.

You need to start getting friendly with the data. Query more, dig into the data and see more meanings, correlate the business with the data and try to see the business in the data. More than that, transfer your atomic vision to the holistic one. This means trying to find the data sets from the data rows. You need to start having a vision of the data. The atomic approach actually starts from a lack of vision of the data. Using the typical approach of development in the database stems from a total neglect of the most intimate aspect of the database, the nature of data. The nature of data is holistic and set-oriented.

Let's go back to the exercise. This exercise can be solved in many ways. I picked one solution for the atomic approach and one solution for the holistic approach. Let's investigate the atomic approach. Begin by looking at Listing 6-9 to see the code for SQL Server.

Listing 6-9. Display Products, Atomic Style, in SQL Server

```
CREATE PROCEDURE Get_Products_Atomically
AS
BEGIN
  DECLARE @v_Product_Id NUMERIC (10, 0), @v_Prev_Product_Code NVARCHAR (5);
  DECLARE @v_First_Name NVARCHAR (30), @v_First_Product_Code NVARCHAR (200)
  DECLARE @v_Current_Name NVARCHAR (30), @v_Min1_Product_Id NUMERIC (10, 0);
  DECLARE @v_Previous_Name NVARCHAR (30), @v_Product_Code NVARCHAR (200);
  DECLARE @v_Min_Product_Id NUMERIC (10, 0), @v_Make_Flag INT;
  DECLARE @v_Products TABLE(Product_Id INT, Current_Name NVARCHAR (30),
  Previous_Name NVARCHAR (30), Product_Code NVARCHAR (5));
  SELECT @v_Min_Product_Id = MIN (Product_Id) FROM Products;
  SELECT @v_Min1_Product_Id = MIN (Product_Id)
  FROM Products WHERE Product_Id > @v_Min_Product_Id;
  SELECT @v_First_Name = Name FROM Products
WHERE Product_Id = @v_Min_Product_Id;
  SELECT @v_First_Product_Code = Product_Code
FROM Products WHERE Product_Id = @v_Min_Product_Id;
  INSERT INTO @v_Products (Product_Id, Current_Name, Product_Code)
  SELECT Product_Id, Name,
  CASE WHEN Make_Flag = 1 THEN NULL ELSE Product_Code END
AS Product_Code
  FROM Products WHERE Product_Id = @v_Min_Product_Id;
```

```
DECLARE c_Products CURSOR FOR
SELECT Product_Id, Name, Product_Code, Make_Flag FROM Products
WHERE Product_Id > @v_Min_Product_Id
ORDER BY 1;
OPEN c_Products;
FETCH NEXT FROM c_Products
INTO @v_Product_Id, @v_Current_Name, @v_Product_Code, @v_Make_Flag;
WHILE (@@FETCH_STATUS = 0)
BEGIN
        IF (@v_Min1_Product_Id = @v_Product_Id)
        BEGIN
                SET @v_Previous_Name = @v_First_Name;
                IF (@v_Make_Flag = 1)
                        SET @v_Prev_Product_Code = @v_First_Product_Code;
                ELSE
                        SET @v_Prev_Product_Code = @v_Product_Code;
                INSERT INTO @v_Products (Product_Id, Current_Name,
                Previous_Name, Product_Code)
                SELECT @v_Product_Id, @v_Current_Name, @v_Previous_Name,
                @v_Prev_Product_Code
                SET @v_Previous_Name = @v_Current_Name;
        END
        ELSE
        BEGIN
                IF (@v_Make_Flag = 0)
                        SET @v_Prev_Product_Code = @v_Product_Code;
            INSERT INTO @v_Products (Product_Id, Current_Name, Previous_Name,
            Product_Code)
            SELECT @v_Product_Id, @v_Current_Name, @v_Previous_Name,
            @v_Prev_Product_Code
            SET @v_Previous_Name = @v_Current_Name;
            SET @v_Prev_Product_Code = @v_Product_Code;
        END
        FETCH NEXT FROM c_Products
        INTO @v_Product_Id, @v_Current_Name, @v_Product_Code, @v_Make_Flag;
END;
CLOSE c_Products;
DEALLOCATE c_Products;
SELECT * FROM @v_Products
END
GO
```

Let's analyze the logic, step by step.

1. You store in two variables: the product identifiers for the
   first product and the next product. See the variables
   @v_Min_Product_Id and @v_Min1_Product_Id.

2. You store the name and product code for the first product. See the variables @v_First_Name and @v_First_Product_Code.

3. You add the first product into the table variable. See the table variable @v_Products.

4. You open the cursor with all the products apart from the first one. See the cursor named c_Products.

5. For the second product (the first one in the cursor, equal with the variable @v_Min1_Product_Id), you set up the previous name and you check the flag. If the flag is set to 1, the previous code is the first product code. Otherwise, the previous code is the current product code. You add the data using the variables into the table variable and set the previous name to current name.

6. If there is another product apart from the second one (the first one in the cursor), you check the flag. If it is set to 0, the previous product code becomes the current product code. Add the data to the results table and set up the values for the @v_Previous_Name and @v_Prev_Product_Code.

7. Select the data from the table variable, @v_Products.

Let's analyze the SQL Server solution for the atomic approach more deeply. The Oracle solution is similar but even more procedural!

A Mixed Approach

The solution in Listing 6-9 is very consistent and logical, in strong correlation with the principles of classic structured programming. However, the solution is not purely atomic, as in all of the preceding atomic examples. You are developing a mixed solution because you are using a table variable. The implementation for this example is half-atomic and half-holistic. The table variable is firstly populated in a holistic manner, in a set-oriented style. Then, using the atomic way, a cursor is opened and the table is updated. This is a kind of **mixed approach** and it is better than a completely atomic approach.

This kind of development, this mixed approach and this partially holistic and partially atomic implementation, is very close to the classic SQL Server style of development, in which a table, either a table variable or a temporary table, is manipulated several times until it gets the proper data.

The temporary table is very common in SQL Server, but it's not used much in Oracle. The temporary table or even the variable of type table, or a record or a collection if we look into the garden of Oracle, can be very useful and is part of development. Sometimes they are combined in a mixed approach, like in this example, and things get handled partially holistically in data sets and atomically afterwards. One solution is to partially generate a data set in a structure like a temporary table or an array and populate that structure. Afterwards, you can update the data generated in the temporary table and handle the rest of the logic atomically. This is what you did here.

This mixed approach is an example of a semi-classic procedural approach that is used to generate the results set according to the requirements. This is what most students and application developers do in the database: structured programming and the use of the atomic development approach. The rows in the source table are taken in the cursor row by row and handled atomically: various conditions are checked against the variables stored row by row. In the Oracle version, things are quite similar; however, the objects are even more procedural than in SQL Server because they use real structures (called records) and arrays. The SQL Server table variable is a simpler structure and it is close to SQL; the Oracle types are more procedural. The meaning and the style are the same; the atomic approach is the same. Actually Transact SQL is defined as being a declarative language while PL SQL is a procedural language. However, the cursor is the same cursor and the atomic style can be present in any of the two languages.

This is the general trend and the preferred style that is used in many databases despite the fact that we can use the other approach, native to the database: the **holistic** approach. We can identify situations where the atomic style needs to be used, because these situations do exist. However, very often (more often than you think) the atomic approach and the procedural style can be avoided and replaced with the holistic approach and the pure SQL style of development.

Table 6-3 shows the results.

Table 6-3. *Sample Product Values*

Product Id	Current Name	Previous Name	Product Code
1	Product 01	NULL	A1
2	Product 02	Product 01	A1
3	Product 03	Product 02	A3
4	Product 04	Product 03	A3
5	Product 05	Product 04	A5
6	Product 06	Product 05	A6
7	Product 07	Product 06	A7
8	Product 08	Product 07	A7
9	Product 09	Product 08	A8
10	Product 10	Product 09	A9

The Holistic Solutions

Let's see the solution of the holistic approach to this problem and analyze it. This is a complete holistic approach. You can compare the two approaches and you can see the differences. From the performance point of view, you can generate larger data sets and compare the timing in both implementations. You will be amazed at the differences.

The holistic approach is so simple compared to the atomic approach! Review Listing 6-10.

Listing 6-10. Display Products, Holistic Style, in SQL Server

```
CREATE PROCEDURE Get_Products_Holistically
AS
SELECT Product_Id, Current_Name, Previous_Name, Product_Code
FROM
(
        SELECT a.Product_Id, p_Current.Name AS Current_Name, p_Previous.Name
        AS Previous_Name,
        CASE WHEN p_Current.Make_Flag = 1 THEN p_Previous.Product_Code ELSE
        p_Current.Product_Code END
        AS Product_Code, 1 AS Type
        FROM
        (
                SELECT Product_Id, ROW_NUMBER () OVER (ORDER BY Product_Id)
                Current_Row_No,
                ROW_NUMBER () OVER (ORDER BY Product_Id) -1 AS
                Previous_Row_No
                FROM Products
        ) a INNER JOIN Products p_Current ON (p_Current.Product_Id =
        a.Product_Id)
        INNER JOIN
        (
                SELECT Name, Product_Id, Product_Code, ROW_NUMBER () OVER
                (ORDER BY Product_Id) Row_No FROM Products
        ) p_Previous ON (p_Previous.Row_No = a.Previous_Row_No)
        UNION
        SELECT TOP 1 Product_Id, Name AS Current_Name, NULL AS Previous_Name,
        CASE WHEN Make_Flag = 1 THEN NULL ELSE Product_Code END AS Product_
        Code, 0 AS Type
        FROM Products
        ORDER BY Type, Product_Id
) A
GO
```

Just one select statement for so many things? Is that possible? The answer is yes, a simple select statement solves all of the problems. There is no need for cursors, no need for records or tables or temporary variables to populate, etc. There is no need for an atomic approach; there's no need for a mixed approach. One simple select statement is enough.

First, please compare the results. For that, you should execute the store procedures in SQL Server. You will see the same results because the logic is the same; only the approaches and styles are totally different.

This is not a simple example. An effort is required to understand it. Look at the data and analyze everything. You should be aware of the set-based operators and functions like Row_Number; see how you take the data from the previous row in direct SQL and not in a cursor. In this scenario, most programmers would choose the atomic approach, even some database programmers. It looks like a case for a cursor and for manipulation. But this example proves that such situations can be solved holistically. You need to have imagination and you need to jump, mentally, from one row to another and get the data.

I like to say that SQL can perform miracles, and this is a good example!

CHAPTER 7

■ ■ ■

Writing SQL vs. Writing Procedurally

This chapter offers more examples of the two styles of development. I will use the same simple design taken from an inventory database: two tables that store products and product types. The design of the tables can be seen in Listing 6-7 in Chapter 6. Don't forget to create the two tables by executing the script in Listing 6-7.

The two styles of development will be illustrated by another opposition, apart from the main one of holistic versus atomic. I am talking about the opposition between SQL code and procedural code. These two approaches are related and similar, but still different.

An Example of an Update

If you take a closer look at the data in the tables, you will notice that there is no description for the products. The purpose of the following exercise is to update the description based on a certain algorithm.

Here is the business description: You want to update the product description in the Products table. In an inventory system (production), product codes have their own significance. According to this, you can see an algorithm for the description based on the code of the type (field Product_Type in the table Product_Types) and the already familiar flag (field Make_Flag from the table Products). If the type starts with the letter C, you should look at the flag. If the flag is 1, you need to concatenate the constant string value DESC plus the code of the product and the code of the type; otherwise you should concatenate the constant DESC plus the code of the product plus the name of the product. If the type is anything else but C, you look at the flag and add the name of the product and the constant if it is 1; otherwise you add the type of the code.

Looking at this description, you can easily see that the author was thinking atomically and procedurally. You can already derive the set of if-else statements, the scalar functions, and a nice cursor! This is the atomic approach.

© Stefan Ardeleanu 2016
S. Ardeleanu, *Relational Database Programming*, DOI 10.1007/978-1-4842-2080-1_7

An Atomic Solution

For this type of request, let's use a pure atomic solution. Create one function named get_type with a parameter of the product identifier. This procedure will return the type based on the flag, one of the two parts of the algorithm. Listing 7-1 shows the function in the Oracle version.

Listing 7-1. Scalar Function, Atomic Style, in Oracle

```
CREATE FUNCTION Get_Type
(
    p_Product_Id INT
)
RETURN VARCHAR2
AS
    v_Type VARCHAR2 (255);
    v_Make_Flag INT;
BEGIN
    SELECT Make_Flag INTO v_Make_Flag FROM Products WHERE Product_Id =
    p_Product_Id;

    IF (v_Make_Flag = 1) THEN
        SELECT t.Product_Type_Code INTO v_Type
        FROM Product_Types t INNER JOIN Products p ON (p.Product_Type_Id =
        t.Product_Type_Id)
        WHERE p.Product_Id = p_Product_Id;
    ELSE
        SELECT t.Name INTO v_Type
        FROM Product_Types t INNER JOIN Products p ON (p.Product_Type_Id =
        t.Product_Type_Id)
        WHERE p.Product_Id = p_Product_Id;
    END IF;

    RETURN (v_Type);
END;
/
```

For a given product, based on the value of the flag, you either generate the type's code from the Product_Types table or the name of the product from the Products table. This is a classic scalar function and the purpose is obvious. This function will be executed in a cursor for all the products later. This is one of the most common scenarios of work for an application developer.

This is the same pattern described in Chapter 6. The cursor and the set of scalar functions and their walk through the cursor allow row division.

After building this function, the logic will continue with the update procedure. Listing 7-2 shows the procedure.

Listing 7-2. Update Description in a Cursor in Oracle

```
CREATE PROCEDURE Upd_Products_Desc_Atomic
AS
        v_Product_Id INT;
        v_Product_Type_Code VARCHAR2 (5);
        v_Product_Code VARCHAR2 (5);
        v_Description VARCHAR2 (255);
        v_Generated_Type VARCHAR2 (255);
        v_rid ROWID;
        CURSOR c_Get_Products IS
        SELECT Product_Id, rowid FROM Products FOR UPDATE OF Product_
        Description;
BEGIN
        OPEN c_Get_Products;
        LOOP
                EXIT WHEN c_Get_Products%NOTFOUND;
                FETCH c_Get_Products INTO v_Product_Id, v_rid;
                v_Generated_Type := Get_Type(v_Product_Id);
                SELECT p.Product_Code, t.Product_Type_Code INTO v_Product_
                Code, v_Product_Type_Code
                FROM Products p INNER JOIN Product_Types tON (p.Product_
                Type_Id = t.Product_Type_Id)
                WHERE p.Product_Id = v_Product_Id;
                v_Description := 'DESC_';
                IF (SUBSTR (v_Product_Type_Code, 1, 1) = 'C') THEN
                        v_Description := v_Description || v_Product_Code;
                END IF;
                IF SUBSTR (v_Description, LENGTH (v_Description), 1) <> '_'
                THEN
                        v_Description := v_Description || '_';
                END IF;
                v_Description := v_Description || v_Generated_Type;
                UPDATE Products
                SET Product_Description = v_Description
                WHERE rowid = v_rid;
        END LOOP;
        COMMIT;
        CLOSE c_Get_Products;
END;
/
```

The steps are quite clear.

1. Declare the cursor for the table Products with the option of updating the description, which is your goal.

2. Calculate the generated type using the function created before.

3. Use a string inside the cursor for the description and start concatenate to that string (v_Description).

4. Get the code of the product and the product code type for the given product from the cursor.

5. If the first letter of the type code is the letter C, add the product code to the description string.

6. Add the generated type and finalize the description for the given product inside the cursor.

7. Update the description with the calculated value of the description for the given product.

8. That will happen for all products. Finally, the table will be updated.

This is the classic atomic and procedural approach. It is so complicated compared to a simple update. Yet the atomic approach is all too familiar to application developers, who follow it instinctively if they are not warned from the beginning (ideally, in college) that they should write their code in a different way if they are inside a relational database.

A Holistic Solution

There's an easier way! Maybe the developer reads the business description in a holistic manner and not in an atomic one, In this case. the holistic solution will be used, which is actually trivial for a SQL developer. See it in Listing 7-3.

Listing 7-3. Update Product Description, Holistic Style, in Oracle

```
CREATE PROCEDURE Upd_Products_Desc_Holistic
AS
BEGIN
        UPDATE   Products
        SET Product_Description = (SELECT
                CASE WHEN Products.Make_Flag = 1 AND SUBSTR (t.Product_Type_
                Code, 1, 1) = 'C'
                        THEN 'DESC_' || Products.Product_Code || '_' ||
                        t.Product_Type_Code
                WHEN Products.Make_Flag = 0 AND SUBSTR (t.Product_Type_
                Code, 1, 1) = 'C'
                        THEN 'DESC_' || Products.Product_Code || '_' ||
                        t.Name
                WHEN Products.Make_Flag = 0 AND SUBSTR (t.Product_Type_
                Code, 1, 1) <> 'C'
                        THEN 'DESC_' || t.Name
                WHEN Products.Make_Flag = 1 AND SUBSTR (t.Product_Type_
                Code, 1, 1) <> 'C'
```

```
                    THEN 'DESC_' || t.Product_Type_Code
            END
    FROM Product_Types t WHERE t.Product_Type_Id = Products.Product_
    Type_Id);
    COMMIT;
END;
/
```

Here you see the power of the case statement. This statement can successfully replace the if-else statement in simple SQL. Notice how the simple update statement does everything: it generates the descriptions according to the algorithm and updates the columns. Why complicate things using sophisticated classic methods? Use the power of SQL, a dedicated language for relational databases!

You can easily understand the algorithm from the SQL statement defined in the holistic approach. You can see the conditions specified in the when clause of the case statement. Nothing is secret or difficult in this update statement.

Listing 7-4 shows the holistic approach for SQL Server. Notice how the two approaches are almost identical.

Listing 7-4. Update Description, Holistic Style, in SQL Server

```
CREATE PROCEDURE Upd_Products_Desc_Holistic
AS
BEGIN
    UPDATE Products
    SET Product_Description =
            CASE WHEN dest.Make_Flag = 1
AND SUBSTRING(t.Product_Type_Code, 1, 1) = 'C'
                                        THEN 'DESC_' + dest.Product_Code +
                                            '_' + t.Product_Type_Code
                            WHEN dest.Make_Flag = 0
AND SUBSTRING (t.Product_Type_Code, 1, 1) = 'C'
                        THEN 'DESC_' + dest.Product_Code + '_' + t.Name
                            WHEN dest.Make_Flag = 0
AND SUBSTRING (t.Product_Type_Code, 1, 1) <> 'C'
                                        THEN 'DESC_' + t.Name
                            WHEN dest.Make_Flag = 1
AND SUBSTRING (t.Product_Type_Code, 1, 1) <> 'C'
                                    THEN 'DESC_' + t.Product_Type_Code
                END
    FROM Products dest INNER JOIN Product_Types t
ON (t.Product_Type_Id = dest.Product_Type_Id);
END
GO
```

Let's look at the two procedures in Oracle and SQL Server. See how the code is very similar. This is the advantage of portability. Things are almost the same because SQL is almost the same. Working in SQL and holistically offers you a great advantage.

However, the most important reason for a holistic approach is performance. The other perks are secondary. Performance, portability, simplicity of code, and the fact that the data set is the keyword that defines a relational database; these are enough reasons for an application developer to start rethinking his code in a database.

The Power of a Union

I will continue to analyse and compare the two styles of development. The atomic style is highly general and the holistic style is clearly particular. But the particularity of the holistic style comes directly from the development battlefield: the relational database.

Let's consider a situation that might occur in specific systems where the goal is to move data between classic systems. New data is added to the target from various sources according to certain business conditions. These various conditions can be specified via procedural means like if...then...else statements. Very often, however, the same logic can be implemented by a union operation.

Taking a SQL-Based Approach

Instead of using a variety of if-else and insert statements, you can use one insert statement based on a union. This is not a surprise considering that a union is a combination of data sets. The meaning of an if-else in this context is one of adding data to one target from various sources based on certain conditions.

I want to clarify the concepts once more. There are two oppositions that I want to analyze. The first opposition is the one between atomic and holistic styles. The second one is the opposition between SQL code and procedural code. In most cases, a holistic style is correlated with a SQL, non-procedural style. However, there are situations when the style can be holistic and implemented partially procedurally and, vice versa, the atomic implementation can be implemented partially atomically.

You should be aware that the topic of discussion now is related to the SQL versus procedural code. I am not necessarily referring to the opposition of atomic versus holistic. **The approach can be holistic, but even the holistic approach can be implemented in a SQL style or in a procedural style**. Moreover, the use of a union instead of an if-else is a solution to replace procedural code with SQL code. I don't say it's always better and I don't say it's always recommended, but I encourage you to keep all-SQL solutions in mind.

In a **specific** system, due to the nature of the system of data transfer between various classic systems, it is always better to handle things both holistically and in SQL, not just holistically.

A Specific Example

Imagine that you have geographical criteria for some data and you want to populate a target from various sources. The sources are from different countries and you need to insert various pieces of information based on a condition like country. Instead of using if-else, you can use a union, maybe even union all if you know that the data sets are distinct. Each query block of the union has the respective data set that you would have been writing in the if-else.

The use of union with the use of variables that specify different sets of data can be easily integrated and, very often, large pieces of procedural code (not necessarily atomically, even in the holistic manner) can be replaced with a highly simplified piece of SQL code. For example, any query block of a union can be defined according to a value of a certain application setting. In this way, the query block may be identified either by certain columns that need to satisfy some criteria (like country) but they can also be defined by some variables.

As you now know, it is possible to write holistic and either procedural or SQL, although in most cases the procedural style is associated with the atomic style and the SQL style is associated with the holistic style.

I will show you two different solutions of the same problem, one using the traditional if-else statements (Listing 7-5) and the other using the SQL operator union (Listing 7-6).

Union vs. if-else

Imagine you have a warehouse of SQL templates which is called multiple times in your software application, at the database level of course. The temptation is to avoid the use of procedural code in this warehouse, being a warehouse of SQL statements. If you can use the union instead of if-else, your warehouse will really be a warehouse of SQL statements. I have built this kind of warehouse and it has almost no procedural code inside it, only pure SQL. I found solutions to replace the procedural code.

Assume the same tables with the de-normalized English and French countries and the normalized table. You have data on English and French countries and you need to populate the set of normalized tables like Countries_Languages. You have the countries and the languages; you just need to populate the association tables. Based on variable p_Language_Name, you can add either French languages or English languages or both. Of course the atomic solution can be used. The holistic solution can be made in a more specific procedural way or in a more SQL-oriented manner.

Listing 7-5 shows procedural solution for Oracle.

Listing 7-5. Procedural if-else Solution in Oracle

```
CREATE PROCEDURE Holistic_Full_Tr_Country_Proc
(
  p_Language_Name VARCHAR
)
AS
        v_English_Language_Id INT;
        v_French_Language_Id INT;
        v_Max_CL_Id INT;
BEGIN
        SELECT Language_Id INTO v_English_Language_Id
        FROM Languages WHERE Language_Name = 'English';
        SELECT Language_Id INTO v_French_Language_Id
        FROM Languages WHERE Language_Name = 'French';
```

```
        IF p_Language_Name = 'English' THEN
                DELETE Countries_Languages
                WHERE Language_Id = v_English_Language_Id;
        ELSIF p_Language_Name = 'French' THEN
                DELETE Countries_Languages
                WHERE Language_Id = v_French_Language_Id;
        ELSIF p_Language_Name = 'Both' THEN
                DELETE Countries_Languages
                WHERE Language_Id = v_English_Language_Id;
                DELETE Countries_Languages
                WHERE Language_Id = v_French_Language_Id;
        END IF;
        SELECT MAX(CL_Id) INTO v_Max_CL_Id
        FROM Countries_Languages;
        IF v_Max_CL_Id IS NULL THEN
                v_Max_CL_Id := 0;
        END IF;
        IF p_Language_Name = 'English' THEN
                INSERT INTO Countries_Languages (CL_Id, Country_Id,
                Language_Id, Language_Category)
                SELECT v_Max_CL_Id + CL_Id_Seq.NextVal, c.Country_Id,
                v_English_Language_Id, eec.Language_Category
                FROM English_European_Countries eec INNER JOIN Countries c
                ON (c.Country_Code = eec.Country_Code);
        ELSIF p_Language_Name = 'French' THEN
                INSERT INTO Countries_Languages  (CL_Id, Country_Id,
                Language_Id, Language_Category)
                SELECT  v_Max_CL_Id + CL_ID_Seq.NextVal, c.Country_Id,
                v_French_Language_Id, eec.Language_Category
                FROM French_European_Countries eec INNER JOIN Countries c ON
                (c.Country_Code = eec.Country_Code);
        ELSIF p_Language_Name = 'Both' THEN
                INSERT INTO Countries_Languages (CL_Id, Country_Id,
                Language_Id, Language_Category)
                SELECT v_Max_CL_Id + CL_ID_Seq.NextVal, c.Country_Id,
                v_English_Language_Id, eec.Language_Category
                FROM English_European_Countries eec INNER JOIN Countries c
                ON (c.Country_Code = eec.Country_Code);
                INSERT INTO Countries_Languages (CL_Id, Country_Id,
                Language_Id, Language_Category)
                SELECT v_Max_CL_Id + CL_ID_Seq.NextVal, c.Country_Id,
                v_French_Language_Id, eec.Language_Category
                FROM French_European_Countries eec INNER JOIN Countries c ON
                (c.Country_Code = eec.Country_Code);
        END IF;
        COMMIT;
END Holistic_Full_Tr_Country_Proc;
/
```

The logic is very clear. Based on the language (English, French or both), the data for that language in the normalized table Countries_Languages is deleted and replaced with the data from one reporting table or the other or both. It is a classic if-else statement, nothing else. A lot of programmers will solve this problem in this way, especially application developers. This is a pure procedural solution, and fortunately a holistic solution. This exercise could have been made atomically using a cursor and that would have been the worst scenario.

Now I want to show that sometimes simple SQL statements are enough and the quantity of procedural code can be completely minimized. There is a lot of code in this procedure. Imagine hundreds of pieces like this everywhere in the software application within the database. Let's replace them with pure SQL code; instead of 10,000 lines of code, you will have 3,000, for example. In most cases, the performance will be better.

Listing 7-6 shows the SQL-based solution

Listing 7-6. Holistic SQL Solution in Oracle

```
CREATE PROCEDURE Holistic_Full_Tr_Country_SQL
(
  p_Language_Name VARCHAR
)
AS
BEGIN
        DELETE Countries_Languages dest
        WHERE EXISTS
        (
                SELECT 1 FROM Languages lang
                WHERE lang.Language_Name = p_Language_Name
AND   p_Language_Name IN ('English', 'French')
                AND lang.Language_Id = dest.Language_Id
        )
        OR EXISTS
        (
                SELECT 1 FROM Languages lang
                WHERE lang.Language_Name IN ('English', 'French')
AND lang.Language_Name = 'Both'
                AND lang.Language_Id = dest.Language_Id
        );
        INSERT INTO Countries_Languages (CL_Id, Country_Id, Language_Id,
        Language_Category)
        SELECT v_Max_CL_Id + RowNum AS CL_Id, Country_Id, Language_Id,
        Language_Category
        FROM
        (
                SELECT c.Country_Id, eec.Language_Category,
                (SELECT COALESCE(Max(CL_Id) , 0)
FROM Countries_Languages) AS v_Max_CL_Id,
                (SELECT Language_Id FROM Languages
```

111

```
WHERE Language_Name = 'English') AS Language_Id
                FROM English_European_Countries eec INNER JOIN Countries c ON
                (c.Country_Code = eec.Country_Code)
                WHERE p_Language_Name IN ('English', 'Both')
                UNION
                SELECT c.Country_Id, eec.Language_Category,
                (SELECT COALESCE(Max(CL_Id) , 0)
FROM Countries_Languages) AS v_Max_CL_Id,
                (SELECT Language_Id FROM Languages WHERE Language_Name =
                'French') AS Language_Id
                FROM French_European_Countries eec INNER JOIN Countries c ON
                (c.Country_Code = eec.Country_Code)
                WHERE p_Language_Name IN ('French', 'Both')
        ) lf;
        COMMIT;
END Holistic_Full_Tr_Country_SQL;
/
```

As you can see, this logic contains one delete statement and one insert statement.
The reason is simple: SQL contains a lot of "procedural" facilities, almost all of them set-
oriented. If you understand the power of SQL and you understand the concept of the data
set, you can use its strength properly. The code is much simpler and more readable. The
performance is much better because SQL is set-based and is very fast and native when
working with data sets, which is what you are doing when you are inside a database.

Write Accurate Code First

First and foremost, the programmers need to write correctly. Then they should improve
their SQL. For that, there are many techniques and methods, starting with a continuous
process of rewriting for the SQL itself and continuing with a lot of features and techniques
for the database engine. They can work with the DBAs of course. At this level, the
developers need to know how to read an execution plan; they need to be able to see the
statistics and eventually gather new ones at various levels, etc.

Embedded SQL vs. Dynamic SQL

I still remember the first time I saw the use of dynamic SQL. It was fascinating to see how
to concatenate and add more and more filter conditions to a string. The filter conditions
were dynamically generated by the user, so there was a good reason for the use of
dynamic SQL. The context was one of a report; the conditions in the report contained
many parameters, the filter conditions. The string continued to grow and grow, becoming
a nice and relevant SQL statement. Finally, the concatenation ended, the string was
executed, and the results set were displayed.

The Normal Approach

Sometimes you want to query a table but you don't know exactly which table: it depends on the execution context. You need to select from the unknown and that is not quite normal, is it? In these cases, when uncertain things are waiting at the door of execution, you may consider the use of **dynamic SQL**.

There are two types of SQL, embedded or dynamic. Embedded SQL is normal SQL, a clear and fair statement or set of statements, written as such and interpreted as such, clearly compiled and determined before the execution. If everything goes fine with the compilation step and the syntax of the statements, the semantics of the statements are checked, and the primary and basic elements of the statements are consistently determined. Errors and other surprises might occur during execution, but all these are part of the execution context.

Normally, all the good developers will try to use embedded SQL as much as is possible; they should be confident in the separation between compilation phase and execution phase as two distinct phases that should be analyzed separately and chronologically. If nothing is uncertain at runtime, embedded SQL is an absolute favorite.

Uncertainty at Runtime

However, sometimes the execution contains questions. Let's consider the example of selecting in a table, or updating the table in a certain way. You don't know the name of the table when you build the logic: it might change at runtime. In these cases, you build a string containing all the known elements of the statement and the unknown elements of the statements specified as parameter for the string. After that, the string is generated and executed. The string will become known at execution time so the compilation and execution will be made at execution time. This is a reason for concern because the execution will take the burden of compilation and its impact may be infinitely more severe. This is the main reason why the use of dynamic SQL is to be avoided. It is always better to solve the basic problems of parsing before execution. No one wants to check the syntax and the semantics of the statements at execution time.

The Use of SQL Generators

One of the data migration interfaces I used to work on happened to have large lists of attributes that should have been updated quite often. The statement was pretty much the same but it contained, of course, different variables, like the attributes to be updated. Therefore, it was a repetitive code and it could have been transformed into dynamic SQL. I preferred to avoid this, but I couldn't. I used dynamic SQL but I kept it separate in what I named a list of SQL generators. That list contained many strings that concatenated constants like keywords and variables like columns from tables. I had many lists and I kept them safely, but I did not add them into the software application. These lists were executed and the content of the lists were sets of embedded SQL statements. These statements were copied into the software applications. In this way, the logic was consistent and classic, containing only embedded SQL. If there was an error, I knew exactly where it was; this was another reason for the embedded SQL.

Finding and locating the errors when using dynamic SQL is an extremely difficult task. You need to dig like dog to get the exact place of the error and start the debug activity. If anything changed, I could use the SQL generators to generate everything again.

This is an example of where dynamic SQL is a good choice, when it is acting like a shadow in the back of the actual code. No one knows it exists! I believe it is better this way.

An Example

Imagine you have more reporting tables, not just English and French but 50 reporting tables. You want to periodically generate the data in the 50 tables from the normalized table. You might write a stored procedure to update the 50 tables and use embedded SQL, or you might write a string and execute it in a cursor, changing the name of the country and populating every country from the 50 tables in the cursor. In the first case, you need to maintain the file with the set of 50 embedded SQL statements, which could be time-consuming. Using dynamic SQL, you don't need to do anything, but you may lose the clarity and the significance of the code. Happily, there is a third option: to use these strings as part of the backup logic (metadata logic), to use these strings as SQL generators and execute them to generate the real files of the software.

First, let's add one column to the table Languages. Let's add some data too. Listing 7-7 shows the changes.

Listing 7-7. Update the Design

```
ALTER TABLE Languages
ADD Language_Table_Name VARCHAR(30);
UPDATE Languages
SET Language_Table_Name = 'English_European_Countries'
WHERE Language_Id = 2;
UPDATE Languages
SET Language_Table_Name = 'French_European_Countries'
WHERE Language_Id = 3;
```

There are two reporting tables: one for the English language and one for the French language. These tables are linked to the language so you add this information to the Languages tables. More reporting tables will follow: this information will be updated in the Languages table. If you create a reporting table for Spanish tomorrow, the name of the table will populate the row with the Spanish language. In this way, the table Languages will contain both data and metadata information and will double its utility. Rebuild the data in Countries_Languages and add the initial script and the changes reflected in the initial script (Listing 5-3).

The update above allows you to see data and metadata information in one place and allows you to use dynamic SQL. The table Languages contains the rows 2 and 3 with the values English_European_Countries and French_European_Countries. They are values in the "business" table so they are data. On the other hand, these values correspond to objects in the database, respectively to the tables with the same names. Therefore, they are metadata. This is a common scenario for dynamic SQL, trying to generate your own set of metadata and use it for various purposes. The set of custom metadata allows the developer to generate SQL logic, especially if things are repetitive. This logic can be hidden in dynamic SQL or it can be revealed in embedded SQL and the mechanism for embedded SQL can be separated in a parallel logic. I prefer the second approach: use metadata and dynamic SQL in a parallel layer to generate and use embedded SQL. At execution time, the software application will only see the embedded SQL.

Let's get back to the example. After recreating the three base table again using the script in Listing 5-3 from Chapter 5, let's see one classic example of dynamic SQL in action. Take a look at Listing 7-8.

Listing 7-8. Dynamic SQL and Holistic SQL Server

```
CREATE PROCEDURE Holistic_Full_Country_Dynamic
AS
        DECLARE @v_Language_Id INT;
        DECLARE @v_Language_Name VARCHAR(50);
        DECLARE @v_Language_Table_Name VARCHAR(30);
        DECLARE @v_SQL_Statement NVARCHAR(1000);
        DECLARE c_Get_Languages CURSOR FOR
        SELECT Language_Id, Language_Name, Language_Table_Name
        FROM Languages
        WHERE Language_Table_Name IS NOT NULL;
BEGIN
        OPEN c_Get_Languages
        FETCH NEXT FROM c_Get_Languages INTO @v_Language_Id, @v_Language_
        Name, @v_Language_Table_Name
        WHILE @@FETCH_STATUS = 0
        BEGIN
 SET @v_SQL_Statement = 'DELETE ' + @v_Language_Table_Name;
 EXECUTE sp_executesql @v_SQL_Statement
 SET @v_SQL_Statement = 'INSERT INTO ' + @v_Language_Table_Name + '
(' + @v_Language_Name + '_CL_Id, Country_Code, Country_Name, Language_
Category)' +
 ' SELECT ROW_NUMBER() OVER (ORDER BY c.Country_Code, cl.Language_Category)
AS CL_Id, c.Country_Code,
        c.Country_Name, cl.Language_Category
        FROM Countries_Languages cl INNER JOIN Languages l ON (l.Language_
        Id = cl.Language_Id)
        INNER JOIN Countries c ON (c.Country_Id = cl.Country_Id)
        WHERE l.Language_Name = ''' + @v_Language_Name + ''''; 
        EXECUTE sp_executesql @v_SQL_Statement
 FETCH NEXT FROM c_Get_Languages INTO @v_Language_Id, @v_Language_Name,
@v_Language_Table_Name
        END
        CLOSE c_Get_Languages
        DEALLOCATE c_Get_Languages
END
GO
```

115

Listing 7-8 is dynamic SQL! It is a special kind of programming and it has a certain degree of popularity. I was a fan of dynamic SQL at the beginning but I'm not anymore. Anyway, dynamic SQL is very useful and of great help in certain situations. Let's look at the code: it seems a bit like a Morse code, doesn't it? Of course, you can always print the strings before executing anything in order to understand the meanings; this is what we all do when we have issues.

The Explanation

In this example, there are just two reporting tables. You generated and executed one delete and one insert statement for two tables. This is not a serious economy in code. However, imagine 20 reporting tables and you generate one insert statement and one delete statement instead of twenty. The amount of code will be reduced to a minimum level. The procedure will have 20 lines instead of 200 lines. This is one consequence of dynamic SQL. The length of the code is many times smaller but so is the meaning. Not too many people will understand it. They will guess; they will print various strings, the final string or intermediates; it will be a battle for understanding. What is most important thing when you look at the code? Is it the length of the code? Are you happy to see one procedure with 10 lines but no meaning? Or are you happy to see one procedure with 100 lines but a clear meaning? (There are no general answers to these questions.)

If you execute the procedure above, you will populate the French and English reporting tables. You will see the same data as in Chapter 5 after executing the procedure Atomic_Full_Transfer_Country for both parameters, English and French (see the values). There are five English countries and two French ones.

You can choose to use embedded SQL and to explicitly specify all the tables and objects. The logic will contain everything. With embedded SQL, you see what you execute, you understand everything, and you can catch the errors, if any. The handle errors procedure generator will take you to the error and you can safely debug everything. With dynamic SQL, it is extremely difficult sometimes to identify the place with the error. This is another disadvantage of dynamic SQL.

However, the use of dynamic SQL can be extremely useful, even apart from the classic situation of uncertain things at runtime. Dynamic SQL can be used in a parallel layer; let's call it generator.

Let's take the example above. Let's change that code and remove the essential call to the string, sp_executesql, and replace it with a simple print. For simplicity, you will just print the string instead of saving it directly for example in a custom metadata table with SQL generators.

The new procedure is similar to the previous one but with a major difference. Review the script first. You can see it in Listing 7-9.

Listing 7-9. Dynamic SQL Generator in SQL Server

```
CREATE PROCEDURE Holistic_Full_C_Generator
AS
        DECLARE @v_Language_Id INT;
        DECLARE @v_Language_Name VARCHAR(50);
        DECLARE @v_Language_Table_Name VARCHAR(30);
        DECLARE @v_SQL_Statement NVARCHAR(1000);
```

```
        DECLARE c_Get_Languages CURSOR FOR
        SELECT Language_Id, Language_Name, Language_Table_Name
        FROM Languages
        WHERE Language_Table_Name IS NOT NULL;
BEGIN
        OPEN c_Get_Languages
        FETCH NEXT FROM c_Get_Languages INTO @v_Language_Id, @v_Language_
        Name, @v_Language_Table_Name
        WHILE @@FETCH_STATUS = 0
        BEGIN
 SET @v_SQL_Statement = 'DELETE ' + @v_Language_Table_Name;
 PRINT @v_SQL_Statement
 SET @v_SQL_Statement = 'INSERT INTO ' + @v_Language_Table_Name + '
(' + @v_Language_Name + '_CL_Id, Country_Code, Country_Name, Language_
Category)' +
 ' SELECT ROW_NUMBER() OVER (ORDER BY c.Country_Code, cl.Language_Category)
AS CL_Id, c.Country_Code,
        c.Country_Name, cl.Language_Category
        FROM Countries_Languages cl INNER JOIN Languages l ON (l.Language_
        Id = cl.Language_Id)
        INNER JOIN Countries c ON (c.Country_Id = cl.Country_Id)
        WHERE l.Language_Name = ''' + @v_Language_Name + ''''; 
        PRINT @v_SQL_Statement
 FETCH NEXT FROM c_Get_Languages INTO @v_Language_Id, @v_Language_Name,
@v_Language_Table_Name
        END
        CLOSE c_Get_Languages
        DEALLOCATE  c_Get_Languages
END
GO
```

The difference is between a **print** instruction and an **execute** instruction. The same string is printed instead of being executed. Consequently, the difference is actually huge. The previous procedure was named Holistic_Full_Country_Dynamic and this one is called Holistic_Full_C_Generator. Now you will execute the last procedure and you will display the data in a new code example. The printed string is the text that should be executed. Instead of executing the string in dynamic SQL, you will generate the text with embedded SQL. That text will actually be the effective logic. Listing 7-10 shows the execution results after calling the last procedure.

Listing 7-10. Execution Results in SQL Server

```
DELETE English_European_Countries
INSERT INTO English_European_Countries (English_CL_Id, Country_Code,
Country_Name, Language_Category)
SELECT ROW_NUMBER() OVER (ORDER BY c.Country_Code, cl.Language_Category) AS
CL_Id, c.Country_Code,
        c.Country_Name, cl.Language_Category
```

```
          FROM Countries_Languages cl INNER JOIN Languages l ON (l.Language_
          Id = cl.Language_Id)
          INNER JOIN Countries c ON (c.Country_Id = cl.Country_Id)
          WHERE l.Language_Name = 'English'
DELETE French_European_Countries
INSERT INTO French_European_Countries (French_CL_Id, Country_Code, Country_
Name, Language_Category)
SELECT ROW_NUMBER() OVER (ORDER BY c.Country_Code, cl.Language_Category) AS
CL_Id, c.Country_Code,
          c.Country_Name, cl.Language_Category
          FROM Countries_Languages cl INNER JOIN Languages l
ON (l.Language_Id = cl.Language_Id)
          INNER JOIN Countries c ON (c.Country_Id = cl.Country_Id)
          WHERE l.Language_Name = 'French'
```

This is amazing. It's so clear and readable! Everyone can understand it. If you have an error, it can be identified correctly and quickly: after the line id you will know exactly where to go to debug. The code is pure SQL, native database code, the same code as before but the difference is that now the code is visible and not hidden. What do you need to do? Take this execution result and add it, create a new procedure and store that in your database. This is the real procedure, containing embedded SQL, and you can see it in Listing 7-11.

Listing 7-11. Generated Procedure in SQL Server

```
CREATE PROCEDURE Holistic_Full_Country_Embedded
AS
DELETE English_European_Countries;
INSERT INTO English_European_Countries (English_CL_Id, Country_Code,
Country_Name, Language_Category)
SELECT ROW_NUMBER() OVER (ORDER BY c.Country_Code, cl.Language_Category) AS
CL_Id, c.Country_Code,
          c.Country_Name, cl.Language_Category
          FROM Countries_Languages cl INNER JOIN Languages l
ON (l.Language_Id = cl.Language_Id)
          INNER JOIN Countries c ON (c.Country_Id = cl.Country_Id)
          WHERE l.Language_Name = 'English';
DELETE French_European_Countries;
INSERT INTO French_European_Countries (French_CL_Id, Country_Code, Country_
Name, Language_Category)
SELECT ROW_NUMBER() OVER (ORDER BY c.Country_Code, cl.Language_Category) AS
CL_Id, c.Country_Code,
          c.Country_Name, cl.Language_Category
          FROM Countries_Languages cl INNER JOIN Languages l
ON (l.Language_Id = cl.Language_Id)
          INNER JOIN Countries c ON (c.Country_Id = cl.Country_Id)
          WHERE l.Language_Name = 'French';
GO
```

The logic in Listing 7-11 is the real procedure and the real logic that should be displayed and executed. The approach is purely holistic and SQL, and the reporting tables are updated from the normalized system: everything is clear and straightforward. If you add two more reporting tables tomorrow, you have two options: you can add the two new insert and delete statements directly, or you can simply update the custom metadata information and execute the generator again. I can copy the text into the procedure and recreate the logic. This is my recommended way of working through these kinds of situations.

The use of dynamic SQL is great and it helps us solve some delicate situations like the one when you want to select from a table but the name of the table is unknown. Today you want to generate the English countries and tomorrow you may want the French countries. The decision is made at runtime by the execution user. In these scenarios, dynamic SQL is a good decision. However, in a scenario where you simply have repetitive code and you have a list of actions that should be generated, like a list of insert statements, you can use dynamic SQL in a parallel layer called generator. That generator will be executed periodically and will be the base for your effective code. The effective code will be pure embedded SQL with all the advantages of embedded SQL. This is the scenario that I recommend in this context.

Other Holistic Solutions

Let's move back to the discussion of the atomic approach and the holistic one. The atomic style is defined in most cases by the use of one or more cursors and the use of variables or records, where the data in the cursor is stored atomically, by the loop through the cursor and whatever manipulation is required. This strategy and style is adopted by many application developers who are not fully aware of the fact that inside a relational database the manipulation should be done per data sets in a holistic manner.

My suggestion in most of the examples is that the holistic approach means solving the problem by using a simple SQL statement. By simple, I do not mean that every solution should be very simple. Actually a SQL statement, like a select statement, can be very complicated and can contain hundreds of lines. The code length, the simplicity or complexity of the statement, is not an argument in itself and, very often, the holistic solution is better than the atomic approach.

Sometimes, however, a simple SQL statement is not enough to solve the problem. Sometimes the data needs to be manipulated and intermediary results should be stored and set before getting the result. Sometimes, to be able to reach the results, you need to do an intermediary update of the data to generate all kinds of identifiers and to perform certain concatenations and calculations. There are so many possible reasons for this data manipulation.

In these situations, a simple SQL statement will not be enough to solve the problem in a holistic manner. However, before you rush off to use the cursor, you can try something else. Let's try temporary tables, either explicit or implicit.

Temporary Tables

The temporary table is very dear to SQL Server developers and not so common for Oracle developers. There are some differences between the statuses of the temporary table in the two systems. This is not relevant in our context. The temporary table is a kind of table that exists in any database system. This is one holistic method for storing intermediates in a data manipulation and is often an alternative to the cursor facility and to the atomic approach. The temporary table can be explicit or implicit, if you consider the with clause, which is used more often in database software development. The temporary table generated by the with clause offers great advantages, one of them being exactly this one: avoiding the atomic approach for a better performance and a holistic data manipulation.

During one of my projects, I was in the position to improve performance. There was a nice, big cursor, like Big Brother. This Big Brother drove the entire process of report generation. To be able to generate that report, a lot of intermediate results were generated before the final result. Of course, the Big Brother was extremely slow and the report was terrible. After some deliberation, I decided a holistic solution was required. Simple SQL was not possible, due to the fact that the data to be manipulated required updates. Therefore, I needed to search for something else.

The with clause is a great feature. I tried it, but it was not enough. So finally I used a classic temporary table instead. The atomic approach was used, not with direct SQL but with a classic temporary table. The table was populated first and updated afterwards based on certain conditions. The difference in performance against the cursor was huge. Even if you use a normal table and not a temporary table, the difference is impressive compared with the cursor and the atomic approach. I know that temporary tables are not loved by everyone. I don't recommend using them often. However, compared to the atomic approach, the temporary table is a better solution because it works holistically. By the way, this solution was, surprisingly, in an Oracle environment and not in the classic SQL Server environment.

We all know that cursors in Oracle have a good performance. Despite all these considerations, the atomic approach remains an abnormal style that should not be used unless a holistic solution is unavailable. This is my opinion and this is what I try to prove in this book.

Table Functions

Another holistic feature is the table function, or a type of function that returns a data set or a similar holistic object. These functions are available in many database systems and they are a better alternative than scalar functions executed in cursors. I want to introduce another example of performance improvement that I did, this time in a SQL Server environment.

There was a complex logic of data transfer between two systems. It was an application very suitable for the holistic approach. In this logic, one portion was very expensive with very poor performance. Analyzing the logic, I noticed the procedural and atomic style; a variety of scalar functions were defined and called everywhere in cursors. The performance was a disaster and, of course, any improvement of any type was not possible, except for the rewrite mechanism, of course! The rewrite procedure is very expensive. Whenever you rewrite the logic, you need to continuously check the results, not just the final but also the intermediate results. It is a difficult work, but the satisfaction when you are done is enormous. So what did I do? I replaced almost all of the scalar functions and cursors with a table function. The table function returns a data set, like a temporary table. Instead of updating all the items in the cursor several times using various scalar functions, I updated the table to be returned in the table function. Instead of acting atomically, I acted holistically. That was the big difference. And the difference in performance was impressive.

One Last Atomic Example

These are just two examples of situations where the holistic approach was implemented using other types of objects like temporary tables, explicit or implicit, or table functions instead of cursors with scalar functions. Whenever you replace an atomic solution, use a simple SQL statement. It will work more often than you expect. If one simple SQL statement cannot solve the problem, because the data set should be updated somehow and the simple SQL select statement is not sufficient, there are other possible solutions like the ones specified above. The atomic approach can be used if the row-by-row functionality is really requested by the logic; this will happen rarely.

Let's see one more example. Let's go back to the set of product tables, the products and their descriptions (see Listing 6-7). Here's the business description: you want to calculate the quantities per type of the product according to an algorithm. For each product, if the type is C, you read the flag. If the flag is set to 1, you take the quantity squared, and if the flag is zero, you take the double the quantity. If the type is D, you look again at the flag and take the quantity squared minus the simple quantity if the flag is positive. You take the triple quantity if the flag is zero.

The same question again: do you see this exercise atomically? Are you already riding on the row like John Wayne in the olden days? Let's see the pure atomic solution, although it is quite clear that this can be easily avoided.

Before executing the procedure, reinitialize the list of products and types. This means running the statements once again from Listing 6-8 from Chapter 6, but not before deleting the products and the associated types.

Listing 7-12 shows the atomic solution in Oracle PL/SQL.

Listing 7-12. Atomic Get Default Quantity in Oracle

```
CREATE PROCEDURE Atomic_Get_Qtty_Per_Type
AS
  v_Product_Type_Code VARCHAR(5);
  v_Make_Flag INT;
  v_Default_Quantity INT;
  v_First_Letter_Type CHAR(1);
  v_Current_Qtty INT;
  v_Current_Qtty_C INT;
  v_Current_Qtty_D INT;
  CURSOR c_Get_Products_Qtty IS
  SELECT pt.Product_Type_Code, p.Make_Flag, p.Default_Quantity
  FROM Product_Types pt INNER JOIN Products p
        ON (p.Product_Type_Id = pt.Product_Type_Id);
```

```
BEGIN
        v_Current_Qtty_C := 0;
        v_Current_Qtty_D := 0;
        v_Current_Qtty := 0;
        OPEN c_Get_Products_Qtty;
        LOOP
                FETCH c_Get_Products_Qtty
                INTO v_Product_Type_Code, v_Make_Flag, v_Default_Quantity;
                EXIT WHEN c_Get_Products_Qtty%NOTFOUND;
        v_First_Letter_Type := SUBSTR(v_Product_Type_Code, 1, 1);
                IF v_First_Letter_Type = 'C' THEN
                        IF v_Make_Flag = 1 THEN
                                v_Current_Qtty := v_Default_Quantity *
                                v_Default_Quantity;
                        ELSIF v_Make_Flag = 0 THEN
                                v_Current_Qtty := 2 * v_Default_Quantity;
                        END IF;
                ELSE
                        IF v_Make_Flag = 1 THEN
                                v_Current_Qtty := v_Default_Quantity *
                                v_Default_Quantity - v_Default_Quantity;
                        ELSIF v_Make_Flag = 0 THEN
                                v_Current_Qtty := 3 * v_Default_Quantity;
                        END IF;
                END IF;
                IF v_First_Letter_Type = 'C' THEN
        v_Current_Qtty_C := v_Current_Qtty_C + v_Current_Qtty;
                ELSE
        v_Current_Qtty_D := v_Current_Qtty_D + v_Current_Qtty;
                END IF;
        END LOOP;
        CLOSE c_Get_Products_Qtty;
        DBMS_OUTPUT.PUT_LINE ('The total default quantity for the products
        with C type is ' || TO_CHAR(v_Current_Qtty_C));
        DBMS_OUTPUT.PUT_LINE ('The total default quantity for the products
        with D type is ' || TO_CHAR(v_Current_Qtty_D));
END;
/
```

This solution is very traditional and I believe there is no need for any explanation. The same procedural logic applies; for each row in the data set with the list of products, you check if the type is C or D, and then you look at the flag and, depending on the value, you calculate one quantity or another. Using a kind of global variable to the cursor (actually two, one for C and one for D), you add the current quantities to either C or D. Finally, the two global variables store the quantities.

After the execution of the procedure, you get the following results:

```
anonymous block completed
The total default quantity for the products with C type is 646
The total default quantity for the products with D type is 30
```

This solution will vary based on the database system. There will be differences between Oracle, SQL Server DB2, and PostgreSQL, for example. The procedural languages are different and you need to familiarize yourself with one or another. However, the procedural languages, despite these differences, are all very similar. A cursor is a cursor, a loop is a loop, the syntax is different but the meaning is the same. The atomic style is the same.

The Holistic Solution

Now let's see the holistic approach for Oracle. Seeing the complicated logic, you might believe is it going to be difficult. Actually it is not, and the famous with clause discussed earlier will transform the previous exercise into a simple SQL statement. Listing 7-13 shows the holistic solution.

Listing 7-13. Holistic Get Default Quantity in Oracle

```
WITH types_quantities AS (
        SELECT SUBSTR(pt.Product_Type_Code, 1, 1) AS Type_Code,
        CASE WHEN p.Make_Flag = 1 THEN p.Default_Quantity * p.Default_
        Quantity
        WHEN p.Make_Flag = 0 THEN 2 * p.Default_Quantity
        ELSE NULL END AS Current_Qtty
        FROM Product_Types pt INNER JOIN Products p
          ON (p.Product_Type_Id = pt.Product_Type_Id)
        WHERE SUBSTR(pt.Product_Type_Code, 1, 1) = 'C'
        UNION ALL
        SELECT SUBSTR(pt.Product_Type_Code, 1, 1) AS Type_Code,
        CASE WHEN p.Make_Flag = 1 THEN p.Default_Quantity * p.Default_
        Quantity - p.Default_Quantity
        WHEN p.Make_Flag = 0 THEN 3 * p.Default_Quantity
        ELSE NULL END AS Current_Qtty
        FROM Product_Types pt INNER JOIN Products p
          ON (p.Product_Type_Id = pt.Product_Type_Id)
        WHERE SUBSTR(pt.Product_Type_Code, 1, 1) = 'D'
                                                                )
SELECT Type_Code, SUM(Current_Qtty) AS Current_Qtty
FROM types_quantities
GROUP BY Type_Code;
```

As you can see, this is a simple SQL statement with the help of the with clause. A similar solution can be offered in SQL Server. However, the with clause may not be implemented yet in all database systems.

The Atomic Solution in SQL Server

Let's see another implementation for this practice using the SQL Server database. You can see it in Listing 7-14.

Listing 7-14. Holistic Get Default Quantity in SQL Server

```
CREATE PROCEDURE Atomic_Get_Qtty_Per_Type
AS
  DECLARE @v_Product_Type_Code VARCHAR(5),
  @v_Make_Flag INT, @v_Default_Quantity INT,
  @v_First_Letter_Type CHAR(1),
  @v_Current_Qtty INT, @v_Current_Qtty_C INT, @v_Current_Qtty_D INT;
  DECLARE c_Get_Products_Qtty CURSOR FOR
  SELECT pt.Product_Type_Code, p.Make_Flag, p.Default_Quantity
  FROM Product_Types pt INNER JOIN Products p
          ON (p.Product_Type_Id = pt.Product_Type_Id);
BEGIN
        SET @v_Current_Qtty_C = 0;
        SET @v_Current_Qtty_D = 0;
        SET @v_Current_Qtty = 0;
        OPEN c_Get_Products_Qtty;
        FETCH NEXT FROM  c_Get_Products_Qtty
        INTO @v_Product_Type_Code, @v_Make_Flag, @v_Default_Quantity;
        WHILE @@FETCH_STATUS = 0
        BEGIN
                SET @v_First_Letter_Type = SUBSTRING (@v_Product_Type_
                Code, 1, 1);
            IF @v_First_Letter_Type = 'C'
            BEGIN
                    IF @v_Make_Flag = 1
                            SET @v_Current_Qtty = @v_Default_Quantity *
                            @v_Default_Quantity;
            ELSE IF @v_Make_Flag = 0
                    SET @v_Current_Qtty = 2 * @v_Default_Quantity;
            END
            ELSE
            BEGIN
                    IF @v_Make_Flag = 1
                            SET @v_Current_Qtty = @v_Default_Quantity
                            * @v_Default_Quantity - @v_Default_Quantity;
                    ELSE IF @v_Make_Flag = 0
                            SET @v_Current_Qtty = 3 * @v_Default_Quantity;
            END
            IF @v_First_Letter_Type = 'C'
                    SET @v_Current_Qtty_C = @v_Current_Qtty_C +
                    @v_Current_Qtty;
```

```
            ELSE
                    SET @v_Current_Qtty_D = @v_Current_Qtty_D +
                    @v_Current_Qtty;
            FETCH NEXT FROM c_Get_Products_Qtty
            INTO @v_Product_Type_Code, @v_Make_Flag, @v_Default_
            Quantity;
    END
    CLOSE c_Get_Products_Qtty;
    DEALLOCATE  c_Get_Products_Qtty;
    PRINT('The total default quantity for the products with C type is '
    + CAST(@v_Current_Qtty_C AS VARCHAR(20)));
    PRINT ('The total default quantity for the products with D type is '
    + CAST(@v_Current_Qtty_D AS VARCHAR(20)));
END;
GO
```

You can easily see the similarities between Oracle and SQL Server, at least in these simple examples of atomic approaches. With this, I want to illustrate the fact that the style is similar even if the approaches are atomic. You can check the results and you should see the same values.

The Holistic Approach in SQL Server

The with clause can be used in SQL Server too. I prefer to use a classic temporary table instead. The reason is that sometimes you should manipulate the data before getting the results and sometimes the with clause can be insufficient. Listing 7-15 shows this last example of the holistic approach.

Listing 7-15. Another Holistic Method in SQL Server

```
CREATE PROCEDURE Holistic_Get_Qtty_Per_Type
AS
BEGIN
        CREATE TABLE #types_and_quantities (Type_Code_Prefix CHAR(1),
        Current_Qtty INT);
        INSERT INTO #types_and_quantities (Type_Code_Prefix, Current_Qtty)
        SELECT SUBSTRING (pt.Product_Type_Code, 1, 1) AS Type_Code_Prefix,
        CASE WHEN p.Make_Flag = 1 THEN p.Default_Quantity * p.Default_Quantity
        WHEN   p.Make_Flag = 0 THEN 2 * p.Default_Quantity
        ELSE NULL END AS Current_Qtty
        FROM Product_Types pt INNER JOIN Products p
          ON (p.Product_Type_Id = pt.Product_Type_Id)
        WHERE SUBSTRING (pt.Product_Type_Code, 1, 1) = 'C';
        INSERT INTO #types_and_quantities (Type_Code_Prefix, Current_Qtty)
        SELECT SUBSTRING (pt.Product_Type_Code, 1, 1) AS Type_Code,
        CASE WHEN p.Make_Flag = 1 THEN p.Default_Quantity * p.Default_
        Quantity - p.Default_Quantity
```

```
        WHEN p.Make_Flag = 0 THEN 3 * p.Default_Quantity
        ELSE NULL END AS Current_Qtty
        FROM Product_Types pt INNER JOIN Products p
          ON (p.Product_Type_Id = pt.Product_Type_Id)
        WHERE SUBSTRING (pt.Product_Type_Code, 1, 1) = 'D';
        SELECT Type_Code_Prefix, SUM(Current_Qtty) AS Current_Qtty
        FROM #types_and_quantities
        GROUP BY Type_Code_Prefix;
END;
GO
```

The difference is that, if the algorithm were even more complicated, this temporary table could have been updated several times and eventually combined with other temporary tables. This approach may not offer the best performance sometimes, but it is a holistic approach. This style of work with temporary tables, if required due to complexity, will very rarely have a lower performance compared to the atomic approach. This is one more reason for using a holistic solution versus a classic atomic and procedural solution.

In the following chapters, I will show more examples to illustrate the two styles of development.

CHAPTER 8

■ ■ ■

Row Triggers and the Need for Atomic Solutions

Any relational database has a variety of logical and procedural objects, some of them quite classic and inherited from other languages, like the scalar function or stored procedure. The scalar function is clearly oriented per row, so it is an atomic object. Apart from the traditional objects, there are database-specific objects, and the **trigger** is maybe the most common one. As you probably know, there are many types of triggers, such as statement triggers and row triggers. In a way, the row trigger is very similar to the scalar function, because it is a row-oriented object. In this chapter, you will see how row triggers work and how they move the context to the row level whether we like it or not.

The Use of Row Triggers

When learning database programming languages like PL SQL or Transact SQL, the programmers start with the basics and finish with the set of procedural objects like functions and procedures. The latter are well known from the classic languages so they can understand them relatively quickly. However, soon after learning these types of procedural objects, the programmers learn about a new type of object, specific to databases and especially specific to tables: triggers.

The Seduction

The developer can be seduced by the idea of implicit and automatic execution of the trigger. The main difference between a trigger and a stored procedure resides in execution. A stored procedure is always executed manually and you have full control over the execution, which means you know exactly when you execute it, but you can't say the same thing about the trigger. The most common type of trigger, the table trigger, is always executed indirectly and automatic based on a certain event in the table. These events are generally DML statements. Consequently, you can have insert, update, or delete triggers. The trigger is a dependent object because it is linked to the table. In a way, the trigger is like a constraint, a similar type of object. Moreover, you can do very complex data manipulation inside a trigger and the complexity of a trigger is similar to the complexity of a stored procedure.

© Stefan Ardeleanu 2016

S. Ardeleanu, *Relational Database Programming*, DOI 10.1007/978-1-4842-2080-1_8

The programmers are first seduced by the fact that the execution is automatic, so they can remove this task completely from their head and leave it for the table event. Sometimes automatic execution may be even required.

Afterwards, the programmers learn that a trigger can be a holistic trigger or an atomic trigger, so a *statement* or *row* trigger. Statement triggers act holistically so they are in concordance with the holistic approach. On the other hand, the row trigger is very similar to the scalar function; it is an ideal feature for application developers working inside relational databases. The row triggers are intensively used by them—too intensively, I think.

The Trap of Row Triggers

Row triggers offer the advantage of allowing direct access per every field and every row. Row triggers can be useful. However, the performance of triggers is very poor, so they should normally be avoided. Still, because they are so intimately related to the atomic style of development, they are used intensively in a variety of data-oriented software applications. This is why you can see a large variety of databases filled with row triggers and scalar functions!

One common example is where an artificial identifier should be generated from a sequence. Sequences are a great facility; they're an independent logical object responsible for the generation of numbers starting from a minimum value and growing with a step specified at the time of creation. Sequences are very common and they are an ideal method for artificial numeric generation.

Unfortunately, the application developer likes the combination of the insert trigger and the sequence, or rather a before insert trigger and a sequence. A trigger is also classified by the timing of the event that raises the trigger. The trigger can be before the event or after the event of instead of the event, for views. The before insert triggers and sequences are a common method for the population of artificial identifiers.

Some Example Triggers

Let's go back to Chapter 5 and review the Oracle atomic full transfer, the first exercise. The solution was written in the Listing 5-4. You can see how the identifiers for the English and French languages were generated in the logic in the loop. Now let's change this logic and use some sequences for the key generation for the reporting tables.

You can create either one sequence for both reporting tables or two sequences, one per language. I prefer to create two dedicated sequences. See Listing 8-1.

Listing 8-1. Adding Two Sequences in Oracle

```
CREATE SEQUENCE English_CL_Id_Seq START WITH 1 INCREMENT BY 1
/
CREATE SEQUENCE French_CL_Id_Seq START WITH 1 INCREMENT BY 1
/
```

You will use these sequences to generate the new values for the artificial keys for the reporting tables. For that, you will create two triggers, one per table. Let's see the triggers and then analyze the logic inside, which is actually very simple and classic. See Listing 8-2.

Listing 8-2. Adding Two Row Triggers

```
CREATE TRIGGER English_CL_Id_Tg
BEFORE INSERT ON English_European_Countries
FOR EACH ROW
DECLARE
BEGIN
        IF :new.English_CL_Id IS NULL THEN
                :new.English_CL_Id := English_CL_Id_Seq.nextval;
        END IF;
END;
/

CREATE TRIGGER French_CL_Id_Tg
BEFORE INSERT ON French_European_Countries
FOR EACH ROW
DECLARE
BEGIN
        IF :new.French_CL_Id IS NULL THEN
                :new.French_CL_Id := French_CL_Id_Seq.nextval;
        END IF;
END;
/
```

These two triggers are similar; one is for English and one is for French. These triggers will be executed every time before a new row is inserted into the base table. The new value will be taken from the sequence. Afterwards, it will populate the artificial identifier. This is a very common technique and many application developers use it, especially Oracle developers. Of course, using sequences with triggers mean that the sequence will be the only accepted method for the identifiers population. You can't combine it with any other methods.

A Revised Solution

Let's update the code from Listing 5-4 accordingly and generate the full transfer again. See Listing 8-3.

Listing 8-3. Atomic Full Transfer with Triggers in Oracle

```
CREATE PROCEDURE Atomic_Full_Transfer_Country_t
(p_Language_Name VARCHAR)
AS
  v_Country_Name VARCHAR2(50);
  v_Country_Code VARCHAR2(3);
  v_Language_Category VARCHAR2(10);
```

```
  CURSOR c_Get_Countries (p_Language VARCHAR2) IS
  SELECT c.Country_Name, c.Country_Code, cl.Language_Category
  FROM Countries_Languages cl INNER JOIN Languages l
          ON (l.Language_Id = cl.Language_Id)
  INNER JOIN Countries c
          ON (c.Country_Id = cl.Country_Id)
  WHERE l.Language_Name = p_Language;
BEGIN
  IF p_Language_Name = 'English' THEN
          DELETE English_European_Countries;
  ELSIF p_Language_Name = 'French' THEN
          DELETE French_European_Countries;
  END IF;
  OPEN c_Get_Countries (p_Language_Name);
  LOOP
  FETCH c_Get_Countries
        INTO v_Country_Name, v_Country_Code, v_Language_Category;
  EXIT WHEN c_Get_Countries%NOTFOUND;
        IF p_Language_Name = 'English' THEN
                INSERT INTO English_European_Countries (Country_Code,
                Country_Name, Language_Category)
                VALUES (v_Country_Code, v_Country_Name, v_Language_Category);
        ELSIF p_Language_Name = 'French' THEN
                INSERT INTO French_European_Countries (Country_Code,
                Country_Name, Language_Category)
                VALUES (v_Country_Code, v_Country_Name, v_Language_Category);
        END IF;
  COMMIT;
  END LOOP;
  CLOSE c_Get_Countries;
END Atomic_Full_Transfer_Country_t;
/
```

Compare Listing 8-3 to Listing 5-4. The identifier is not visible anymore: it is updated in the back, by the trigger. If you look at the target tables, you will not see the key because the trigger updates the key.

The Disaster

The technique in Listing 8-3 will be a disaster if medium to large sets of data are to be handled in a data transfer. If you are affecting data sets and using row triggers, you are in a dilemma. Triggers are not visible; you need to search for them.

Imagine a scenario where you are working holistically and set based. You are affecting 100 rows in clean and pure SQL logic. You know that the flow is as fast as it can be. Still, the logic is very slow and you don't know why! Suddenly, you realize that you have a row trigger that changes the entire flow; instead of being a set-based flow and in the holistic style, it is transformed into an atomic flow. Let's rewrite Listing 5-6. You can see it in Listing 8-4.

Listing 8-4. Holistic Full Transfer with Triggers in Oracle

```
CREATE OR REPLACE PROCEDURE Holistic_Full_Transf_Country
(
  p_Language_Name VARCHAR
)
AS
BEGIN
        DELETE English_European_Countries
        WHERE p_Language_Name = 'English';
        DELETE French_European_Countries
        WHERE p_Language_Name = 'French';
    INSERT INTO English_European_Countries (Country_Code, Country_Name,
    Language_Category)
        SELECT c.Country_Code, c.Country_Name, cl.Language_Category
        FROM Countries_Languages cl INNER JOIN Languages l
                ON (l.Language_Id = cl.Language_Id)
        INNER JOIN Countries c
                ON (c.Country_Id = cl.Country_Id)
        WHERE l.Language_Name = p_Language_Name AND p_Language_Name =
        'English';
    INSERT INTO French_European_Countries (Country_Code, Country_Name,
    Language_Category)
        SELECT c.Country_Code, c.Country_Name, cl.Language_Category
        FROM Countries_Languages cl INNER JOIN Languages l
                ON (l.Language_Id = cl.Language_Id)
        INNER JOIN Countries c
                ON (c.Country_Id = cl.Country_Id)
        WHERE l.Language_Name = p_Language_Name AND p_Language_Name =
        'French';
        COMMIT;
END Holistic_Full_Transf_Country;
/
```

This example looks like an example of the holistic style of development. Actually, it isn't! Despite the fact that the logic itself is set-based and holistic, the row triggers change everything and the logic is atomic instead of holistic.

Personally, I rarely use triggers, especially row triggers. They act per row, and they have all the disadvantages of the atomic vision of development. Of course, sometimes they are necessary. You can decide for yourself, but be aware of these disadvantages, and especially be aware of the fact that set-based logic, when associated with row triggers, transforms everything. It's like a mask, and the person behind the mask is revealed by the row trigger!

The Necessity of the Atomic Approach

As mentioned, sometimes the atomic approach is necessary. There are situations when we need to think atomically, to open cursors and move the data at the row level into variables, do various manipulations, etc. The combination of SQL and procedural, and the combination of holistic and atomic, make up database programming. A database programming language is composed of all of them and all the features are needed, more or less often. Still, it is very important to remember that whenever you are developing inside a relational database to just think of rows and columns.

The set-based approach and the holistic style of development refer to tendencies and statistics. In most cases, you should answer your business questions using set-based solutions and holistic answers. However, there are exceptions. The data set is composed of a number of rows and sometimes, to be able to solve your problems, you need to move back to the row level and think atomically. Let's analyze one type of scenario where an atomic solution can be used. Here's the business description:

> *You want to display the list with all the languages and the countries attached, as principal or secondary. You need to concatenate in a string the list of countries separated by commas, for each category.*

This is one of the situations where you can work atomically. Very often, you need to. You may look for set-based facilities like analytics functions (for example, row number). However, if you can't find them, you may think at the cursor and row level.

When is working at the row level actually necessary? From my experience, this occurs when we are forced to do various manipulations row by row and store some intermediate results. I don't believe we can state any rule for the division to be acceptable; things are related to the particularities of the situation. When we need to see things row by row, a simple SQL statement is not enough.

Analyzing the Example

Let's work with an example. There are three tables: one with the languages, one with the countries, and one with their associations. For every language, you have a list of countries, and every language is either principal or secondary for the country. The data is highly normalized. From this design, you need to get a report, a situation per language with two lists. The first list contains all the countries where the language is principal and the second list contains the countries where the language is secondary. For that, you need to be able to move into the tables, in a row-by-row approach, to concatenate the countries, store them somehow, and finally generate the report. This example illustrates the need for the atomic approach in certain situations. Listing 8-5 shows the version for SQL Server.

Listing 8-5. Display a List Atomically in SQL Server

```
CREATE PROCEDURE Atomic_List_Of_Countries
AS
        DECLARE @v_Country_Name NVARCHAR(50);
        DECLARE @v_Language_Category NVARCHAR(10);
```

```
    DECLARE @v_Language_Name NVARCHAR(50);
    DECLARE @v_Language_Id INT;
    DECLARE @v_List_Of_Countries_Main NVARCHAR(4000);
    DECLARE @v_List_Of_Countries_Sec NVARCHAR(4000);
    DECLARE @v_Previous_Language_Name NVARCHAR(50);
    DECLARE c_Get_Languages CURSOR FOR
    SELECT l.Language_Id, l.Language_Name
    FROM Languages l
    WHERE EXISTS
    (
        SELECT 1 FROM Countries_Languages cl
        WHERE cl.Language_Id = l.Language_Id
    )
    ORDER BY 2;
BEGIN
    CREATE TABLE #List_Of_Countries (Language_Name NVARCHAR(50),
    List_Of_Countries_Main NVARCHAR(4000), List_Of_Countries_Sec
    NVARCHAR(4000));
    OPEN c_Get_Languages;
    FETCH NEXT FROM c_Get_Languages
    INTO @v_Language_Id, @v_Language_Name;
    WHILE @@FETCH_STATUS = 0
    BEGIN
    SET @v_List_Of_Countries_Main    = '';
        SET @v_List_Of_Countries_Sec     = '';
        DECLARE c_Get_Countries CURSOR FOR
        SELECT c.Country_Name, cl.Language_Category
        FROM Countries_Languages cl INNER JOIN Countries c
                ON (c.Country_Id = cl.Country_Id)
        WHERE cl.Language_Id = @v_Language_Id
        ORDER BY cl.Language_Category, c.Country_Name;
        OPEN c_Get_Countries;
        FETCH NEXT FROM c_Get_Countries
        INTO @v_Country_Name, @v_Language_Category;
        WHILE @@FETCH_STATUS = 0
        BEGIN
                IF @v_Language_Category = 'MAIN'
                        SELECT @v_List_Of_Countries_Main = @v_List_
                        Of_Countries_Main + @v_Country_Name + ','
                ELSE
                        SELECT @v_List_Of_Countries_Sec = @v_List_
                        Of_Countries_Sec + @v_Country_Name  + ','
                FETCH NEXT FROM c_Get_Countries
                INTO @v_Country_Name, @v_Language_Category;
        END
        CLOSE c_Get_Countries;
        DEALLOCATE c_Get_Countries;
```

```
               IF LEN(@v_List_Of_Countries_Main) > 1
                     SET @v_List_Of_Countries_Main = SUBSTRING (@v_List_Of_
                     Countries_Main, 1, LEN(@v_List_Of_Countries_Main) - 1);
               IF LEN(@v_List_Of_Countries_Sec) > 1
                     SET @v_List_Of_Countries_Sec = SUBSTRING (@v_List_Of_
                     Countries_Sec, 1, LEN(@v_List_Of_Countries_Sec) - 1);
               INSERT INTO #List_Of_Countries (Language_Name, List_Of_
               Countries_Main, List_Of_Countries_Sec)
               VALUES (@v_Language_Name, @v_List_Of_Countries_Main,
               @v_List_Of_Countries_Sec);
               FETCH NEXT FROM c_Get_Languages
               INTO @v_Language_Id, @v_Language_Name;
        END
        CLOSE c_Get_Languages
        DEALLOCATE  c_Get_Languages;
        SELECT * FROM #List_Of_Countries
        DROP TABLE #List_Of_Countries
END
GO
```

Of course, that this could have been done in many ways; this is one of the many possible solutions. Let's analyze the logic in Listing 8-5. Even if the solution is atomic, you are still in the world of data. This means that everything starts from a data set. Let's call it the base data set or the detail data set. The base set is shown in Listing 8-6.

Listing 8-6. Display the Base Data Set in SQL Server

```
SELECT c.Country_Name, cl.Language_Category, l.Language_Name
FROM Countries_Languages cl INNER JOIN Languages l
        ON (l.Language_Id = cl.Language_Id)
INNER JOIN Countries c
        ON (c.Country_Id = cl.Country_Id)
ORDER BY l.Language_Name, cl.Language_Category, c.Country_Name;
```

Let's look at the data because this is the key to the solution. Table 8-1 shows the countries and their languages.

Table 8-1. Countries and Languages

Country Name	Category	Language Name
The Netherlands	MAIN	Dutch
Malta	MAIN	English
United Kingdom	MAIN	English
United States of America	MAIN	English
Switzerland	SECONDARY	English
The Netherlands	SECONDARY	English
France	MAIN	French
Switzerland	MAIN	French
Austria	MAIN	German
Switzerland	MAIN	German
Malta	MAIN	Maltese
Argentina	MAIN	Spanish
Spain	MAIN	Spanish

Listing 8-1's data set is the starting point for the solution. Starting from here, you need to generate the report. You can see a variety of languages and associated countries with the associated category. For example, Malta, UK, and US have English as the main language. Switzerland and Netherlands have English as a secondary language. For a larger list, you need to position in the language and then you need to concatenate the countries based on category (main and secondary). Simple SQL isn't enough because obtaining the list of countries requires row-by-row access and row division.

Reviewing the Solution

Let's see the proposed solution. Start by looking again at Listing 8-5. The overall approach is the following:

1. You declare one cursor for the languages. You store the languages that have at least one country assigned to it. You store from this cursor, for every row, the language name and language identifier.

2. You create a temporary table in the pure SQL Server style to get the results.

3. You declare two variables dedicated to storing the lists of countries, based on category: one for main and one for secondary.

4. For every language, you declare another cursor and use it with the list of countries. For every language, you store the country and the category in dedicated variables.

5. In the second cursor, the inner cursor, you start concatenation and link the countries, separated by a comma.

6. When you're done, you move back to the outer cursor and remove the last comma from the string from both lists.

7. In the outer cursor with the languages, you add the data from the dedicated variables and populate the reporting table.

8. In the end, you display the desired list.

The results are in Table 8-2.

Table 8-2. *The Results*

Language Name	List of Countries Main	List of Countries Sec
Dutch	The Netherlands	
English	Malta, United Kingdom, United States of America	Switzerland, The Netherlands
French	France, Switzerland	
German	Austria, Switzerland	
Maltese	Malta	
Spanish	Argentina, Spain	

Listing 8-5 shows that sometimes you can use the atomic approach. Cursors are a great feature and this example shows why. The cursors, in combination with loops and fetch, allow you to position yourself from one row to another and do various manipulations. I don't deny their utility. What I intend to show almost everywhere in this book is the fact that you need to be aware that you are in a database, you are affecting data sets, and you need to keep in mind the holistic vision first. That does not mean you should not be aware of the possibility of division from data set to data row when necessary.

Wrap-Up on Atomic Operations

Cursors and row-level manipulation are necessary when the business requirements are of a nature that forces you to position at the row level and do various manipulations. These manipulations can be handled by various set-based facilities like row number, but if you don't have such facilities or if you can't find them, you always have the option to use cursors and move the context to the row level.

Sometimes you need to handle things atomically, but you don't need to think atomically unless it's necessary. This is the whole point of this book. In addition to performance, portability, simplicity, and naturalness, it is obvious and normal to think holistically and to think SQL, due to the nature of data.

CHAPTER 9

Final Reflections and Thoughts

I am not a guru. What I am is a passionate and dedicated SQL person. I spent many years in SQL development and I developed my own style. During these years, I gathered many experiences, discovered many ideas, and rediscovered the wheel many times. I know very well that most of the ideas explained here are well known to many professionals all over the world. However, I hope to offer a better view and I hope to clarify some of our realities.

Apart from the distinction between the two styles of development, I want to share some other thoughts and ideas from my experience as a SQL developer. Maybe some developers will follow some of my advice, maybe not. We live in a free world, so every reader of this book can make the best decision in accordance with his personality and, why not, with his style!

The Principle of Division

When considering the holistic approach for your database and deciding to develop accordingly, and depending on the type of system, you should follow the classic principles of programming. Working holistically does not mean ignoring the classic principles of programming, but trying to combine what is most suitable from both worlds.

For example, working holistically does not mean having large procedures with a lot of logic inside. You may have such things due to business requirements, not because of the holistic style of development.

The principle of division, popular in programming and in life, is also available in the holistic approach. This principle states that, if a problem is complex, it can be divided into simpler problems; and these ones can eventually be divided too.

Division may occur over time, not necessarily from the beginning. Very often, we are focused on the general task, the big problem, without being aware of the principle of division. When we are done with the logic and we look at our masterpiece, we realize that we could have divided the logic into many pieces, like functions and procedures.

© Stefan Ardeleanu 2016

S. Ardeleanu, *Relational Database Programming*, DOI 10.1007/978-1-4842-2080-1_9

The Concept of a SQL Template

Considering that you are in a database and you should work holistically, there are many SQL statements to handle and manage. Very often, these SQL statements are similar; sometimes they are not. SQL templates are a good option. In a replication or data migration system, which is a kind of specific software application that is very suitable for the holistic approach, you may consider the use of SQL warehouses. A SQL warehouse is a collection of SQL templates. I use the term *template* because it is used repeatedly with minor changes, which can be various parameters, and I call it *SQL* because it is a pure SQL statement. That collection of statements can embrace a large number of SQL statements that can be executed in one context or another. At execution time, the SQL templates will receive effective values for the parameters.

The holistic approach means the use of SQL. Most of the logic is made up by SQL statements. In a specific system where the goal is always the same (moving data from A to B), the data movement process can be managed in pure SQL. Consequently, the only thing you need to do is to get the set of SQL statements. For better organization, you can gather many SQL statements in the warehouse and call a template from various places in the specific software application.

The SQL warehouse can be placed in a table. It will become data and metadata at the same time. The metadata table can contain many fields that are related to the template and one field with the template itself. The SQL templates are executed using dynamic SQL, of course, in various contexts in the software application.

The custom metadata table is one possible house for SQL templates. The warehouse can also be placed in a stored procedure with a series of parameters. The stored procedure will be executed in one context or another.

I have used both approaches. I prefer the stored procedure because I see only embedded SQL. I see the templates, I can easily read and understand everything, and I can eventually compare various templates. If I use the metadata table, all the templates are hidden. To look into a SQL template, I need to query the table, take the template separately in another window, and debug that template. The procedure is not convenient. But both methods are acceptable and are good places for the SQL template warehouse.

Thinking holistically is the first step, especially in a specific system like an ETL or data migration system. The holistic style and vision are welcome in the classic software system, but some things are atomic due to the nature of the business.

Consider an invoicing system. You are now in an invoice and you are updating that invoice. You are already in one invoice, so the level is close to the atomic level. Consequently, it does not matter too much if the approach is holistic or atomic. But think of the details of the invoice; it's one thing to update 200 details in one action in a holistic manner and another to try to affect every detail in a cursor.

As you can see, even in a classic system, it's recommended to follow the holistic approach, but it's not always necessary. However, it is necessary in a system where the goal is to move data between various systems. In these kinds of software systems, at the database level, you should always consider the holistic approach. You can classify the statements and try to organize them properly. For this reason, you can organize them in SQL warehouses, embedded in either custom metadata tables or stored procedures.

The fact that a large number of SQL templates are grouped in one single place like a stored procedure is a feature close to the classic vision of programming. Based on business criteria, many SQL warehouses can be created in a system. For example, you can have a staging area between the source and the target system. You can have one SQL warehouse for all the templates that are used for the data movement from the source to the staging and you can have another warehouse composed of most SQL templates used for the movement from the staging to the target.

In a specific system where the goal is simply to move data from one system to another, the data should be moved in data sets as much as possible. The main type of statement responsible for the data set flow is the SQL statement. The decision to group the SQL statements according to certain criteria is a good decision and it will increase the level of organization of the system.

Writing Horizontally vs. Vertically

The programming style of development is defined by a set of principles and rules described in the models and paradigms. The style of development is also relative to the area of interest and work. It is one thing to develop mainly in Oracle and another to develop mainly in Java. Our style is influenced by the technologies used in our projects, and our style is dynamic; it may change in time. This is one reason why I am optimistic that some application developers will reconsider their work in the database and try to change something. Even an intention to change is a victory for the database in general and for me in particular.

Working holistically or atomically is part of each person's style of programming in the database. This decision and this tendency is a major component of the style of development. The style is reflected in the code; it's easy to recognize. If you see cursors over cursors for every operation and a variety of scalar functions or row triggers, it means that you are in front of an application developer working in the database in his own way. If you see data sets manipulated holistically almost everywhere, this is the opposite style.

A secondary characteristic of a style of development is the way we effectively write. The aspect of our code is an important component but has its degree of subjectivity. That is why this topic is not regulated and indeed it should not be regulated. We can't force people to write in a certain way, but we can explain that a certain writing rule is better than another one. A procedural object, like a procedure or function, can have hundreds of lines. The most important thing for this object is to work properly. The procedure also needs to be intelligible. Others programmers should be able to understand it. Sometimes we don't even understand our own code! One reason is the way we write.

I will explain using a clear and common example. In the database, there are many SQL statements. Let's imagine one procedure with 10 insert statements, 5 update statements, 7 delete statements, and other procedural logic in it apart from the SQL.

Some programmers write the SQL statements vertically. For example, if you have an insert statement and you have 20 columns, you will have between 40 and 50 lines for this insert statement. Vertical writing means specifying one column per line and effectively writing vertically. If you have 10 insert statements, you may have between 400 and 500 lines for these insert statements. You can see how it can get very confusing.

Let's see an example. Imagine you have one insert statement in a procedure. Listing 9-1 shows two ways to write the insert statement.

Listing 9-1. Writing Insert Statements

```
--Writing vertically

INSERT INTO Countries_Languages (
        CL_Id,
        Country_Id,
        Language_Id,
        Language_Category
        )VALUES (
        14,
        2,
        2,
        'SECONDARY');


-- Writing horizontally
INSERT INTO Countries_Languages (CL_Id, Country_Id, Language_Id,
Language_Category)
VALUES (14, 2, 2, 'SECONDARY');
```

My Reason Against Tools

Imagine you are in a specific system where you have many insert, update, and delete statements, and you write everything vertically. Will you be able to understand anything from the logic? It will be extremely difficult. See the difference in the example above and answer one question. Why would you write an insert statement vertically? Give me one good reason.

The insert statement is one statement. If you declare 10 variables, you may add them in 10 lines, each variable declaration on one line. Every variable is distinct and deserves its own line! In contrast, a column in an insert or a value specified is not a distinct component to be added in distinct lines. One insert statement is one single statement. The purpose is to be able to understand the insert statement. For that, writing horizontally makes it much easier to see and understand what it is about. You can follow each column to each corresponding value; you can check the data types. Eventually, you can check the compatibility. An insert statement, to be intelligible, should be written mostly horizontally.

Another reason for writing an insert statement vertically is the fact that it is the mirror of the tool. Some development tools generate the insert statements vertically by default. Some tools present you with a certain way to write. That does not mean you should write blindly without thinking. Writing SQL vertically is a catastrophe for your logic because it will make your code completely unreadable. For example, in an insert statement, you should be able to follow the link between every column and every associated value. Writing vertically makes this task impossible. The tools should not drive us; we should drive the tools.

Regarding the style in the database, I think writing SQL statements horizontally is extremely important for the readability of our software. We need to understand what we write. The SQL statement is the most important type of statement and we need to understand it exactly. Although it is a matter of form and not substance, it is important. In addition, writing horizontally does not mean writing 30 columns in one line; this will cause the same problems and the same lack of understanding. Writing horizontally means writing the number of columns or expressions that fill the line. The point is to have the proper visibility and to understand the code without needing to move to the right all the time.

Sometimes programmers generate the logic from the tools. They have an initial version, and they update everything after. This is another reason for the existence of unreadable code. If the logic is very simple, you can leave it. If not, it is difficult to work in this style.

Writing vertically also shows a lack of respect for the SQL statement. The developers should understand that the SQL statement is one statement; it's a unit of work. They need to do everything in their power to catch the whole, or as much as possible. A SQL statement can have hundreds of lines even in a horizontal manner.

Writing horizontally is a decision based on reason and not on taste. Some programmers will say it is their taste. Even if this is true, all the arguments for intelligibility are in favor of the horizontal writing of SQL statements. Taste should be a factor of decision for a programmer as long as it is not against reason, don't you think?

Specific Software Applications

A specific (data migration, replication, even ETL) software application is very common nowadays. Most large enterprises have multiple systems and databases that communicate with each other. In a continuous transfer between operational systems, like a replication system or a data migration system, or a transfer between a set of operational systems and an analytics, like in an ETL process, the logic of data transfer between systems is more and more present everywhere.

These kinds of systems should be made by database developers and should not be left in the hands of pure application developers. I know many people may disagree with this categorical statement. I also recognize there is a degree of subjectivity in this statement. Actually, I can rephrase it and affirm that these kind of systems should be made by either specialized database developers or by mixed developers with an open mind—so open that they can write classically in the user interface and write holistically and set-oriented in the database. These application developers, even though they specialize in languages like Java or C++, understand the simpler model of the database; they understand the set-based approach. They are very good programmers, with brilliant and flexible minds, who can make the switch appropriately.

The first condition for this kind of specific system to work properly and to have a good performance is to be written correctly. By having the proper style in a specific system, and adopting the holistic style of development, you can analyze the logic in data sets and search for any weaknesses. There is no such thing as a perfect software system of any type. Consequently, there will always be performance issues.

The holistic style of development means using mostly SQL. The entire data migration system should be composed mainly of SQL statements. The data is transferred, as it should be. Now the programmer can move to the next phase, trying to improve the performance of the SQL itself!

Regarding the SQL itself and the performance, there are so many possibilities that I could fill five books. Improving one SQL statement or improving certain logic composed of mainly SQL statements is a challenging task. Let's cover a few things that must be done.

SQL Itself Can Be Improved

First, let's get a deeper understanding of the SQL paradigm, apart from the language, apart from the business. As mentioned, there are two main goals when dealing with software. First, you need to implement the business. For example, if you want to move some products from an ERP system to a production system, you need to make sure the products are moved correctly. If you have ten products to be moved from the ERP system, you can check them in the target system, attribute by attribute. If everything is accurate, you have successfully completed the first and the most important goal. Once this is done, you can look further and question the performance. Waiting one minute for ten products may be acceptable. Waiting ten minutes for ten products may not be acceptable, even if you see the products in the target. In other words, the second goal is performance. In the database, you can see any performance issues easily by looking at the response times.

If you have a log in the data migration system, you may find steps with performance issues. You can detect the place with the issue. You need to take the SQL or the set of SQL statements separately and investigate. The first phase of the investigation is to check if the SQL was accurate. Let's see some of the performance checks that can be done against the SQL in the database.

- When you have to choose between joins and subqueries, it's generally better to use joins. In most cases, this is possible. An excessive use of subqueries and a replacement of the joins with subqueries will decrease the performance of the SQL statement. In SQL, the same result set can be achieved in many ways. A SQL programmer should know which technique offers better performance. Some things are quite well known, others can be found by looking at the execution plan of the statement.

- The use of unions should be made with caution; always check to see if you can use a union all instead. The union operator always involves a sort operation, which is very expensive. Check that the data sets are grouped in a union and check if there is a need for removal of duplicates. If you know that the data sets in the union are distinct, you can replace the union with union all for much better performance. A union may take five minutes and a union all against the same blocks may take five seconds!

- Avoid a left outer join because the indexes may not work on the tables. Sometimes a left outer join can be avoided or replaced with something else, so add it only if it is really required by the business.

- Use the specific SQL for the vendor if it has better performance than standard SQL. As mentioned, the SQL Server form of update is specific but it has better performance than the more general form with the subquery. Many SQL statements are available in many different forms and you should know if the performance is the same or not.

There are many more tips to cover; this is another topic that deserves a separate space. However, the most important thing is to write clean SQL from the business point of view and from the performance point of view.

The ability to read an execution plan is, of course, crucial. Not all developers know how. But if you want to improve performance, you need to be able to read and understand the execution plan of a SQL statement. If you write clean and you know the basics, you will get good performance.

There are many other things, like indexes, partitions, parallelism, materialized views, and other facilities. These facilities will improve the performance and the developer that knows all them is a true database developer.

Performance, Oh Performance!

Performance is the second goal in the database, the first one being the accurate implementation of the business. All books mention performance. Everyone says that performance is critical. In reality, we rarely think of performance from the beginning. We analyze it later when the software application has been created and is already in production. Consider an invoicing system. We think about the user interface design and the database design; we analyze the invoicing business; but we rarely think seriously about performance. Despite the fact that most professional books recommend that performance should be carefully analyzed from the beginning, we rarely listen. It's the same with our health: we begin to care about our health only after we get sick.

I have read many books about performance and I have worked on this issue many times. I am a contractor, and very often contractors are called in to solve performance issues that have existed for years. There are many techniques for improving performance. I already described some of my interventions on some of my projects. Being able to improve performance is a valuable skill for a professional. You need to have a distinct type of knowledge for it, apart from simple development. In the field of databases, performance is a separate section and the database professionals involved in performance are half developers, half DBAs: they are the doctors of the databases, and they are very appreciated and respected.

As an analogy, the Nordics have the best hearts in the world. Their health is incredible and they are happy nations. I can tell you it is true because I had been in Nordic countries many times. I was amazed by what I saw. First, I am a sports person. I love sports; I play squash and badminton regularly, I like to run, and I also like to watch various sports like tennis and handball. I was even a sports journalist for a short period. As you can see, sports are part of my life. Still, I never imagined that I would find a nation dedicated to sports. But I did in Finland, Sweden, Norway, and Denmark. These nations are healthy nations firstly because they all participate in sports. Everyone runs, everyone bikes, and the pools are full of people of all ages, from children to seniors. Why are they doing so many sports? Not because they are necessarily great fans like me; many of them don't care about professional sports. They are simply doing sports because they care about their body. This applies to diet as well. During my database courses I would eat lunch with my students. They ate only salads; they were not eating much bread. The reason was the same: health (otherwise known as performance).

You just saw how a nation can analyze and take into account performance in their daily activities. Why can't we do the same in our projects? Regarding the database, the first measure we should take is to write correctly in the database. In other words, stop using an inappropriate style of development in our databases. Stop killing performance with cursors over cursors and scalar functions over scalar functions called everywhere, and structures and records and arrays instead of classic and native SQL facilities. We need to stop considering SQL as an additional skill that can be achieved easily by anyone, and instead have more respect for this language. Looking at performance firstly means explaining to the application developers working in our databases that they need to think differently due to the simple fact that they are in a distinct environment, the database, where the main concept and concern is to handle everything in data sets.

Just the First Step

When we write correctly from the beginning, we start with the premise of good performance. This is why I insist on explaining the concepts of the data set and the set-oriented style of development to my students. The young generation of programmers must be aware from the beginning, before they start to write code, that they need to think differently in the database. They must be told this explicitly. It is such a simple solution but it may have very good consequences! Let's imagine for a moment that all data-oriented software applications are written correctly in the databases. I can guarantee that it will be a better world, from a performance point of view.

True SQL specialists need to take SQL statements and improve them; they need to replace a poor syntax with a better one until they get the best SQL. Then the DBAs and the database specialists can enter the scene and add valuable features for performance. The main reasons for poor performance will be eliminated. Of course, this will never happen. I am not naive enough to believe this; it was just a game of imagination.

All of the principles described in this book can be applied to a database where the style of development is the holistic, set-oriented style of development. If the database is written in the atomic style of development, these principles are useless. Consequently, from this perspective, my book is a book about performance, even the first part of it. If you don't write holistically in the database, especially ones that implement specific software applications, you will have poor performance. It is up to you to decide, as a programmer and as a manager of the project, if you really care about the performance of your software application. The game is yours: you should properly learn the rules! The style of the player is always a critical component of the game. Apart from learning the rules, look at the style and choose wisely in concordance with your reason. I offered you good reasons for a certain style, and you can check for yourself whether it makes any difference in terms of performance. The ball is in your court!

Pure SQL is the Way

The main topic of this book is the use of a proper style of development in every layer of a software application. I focused on the relational database, but I believe this applies to other sections in the field of software development. The way we write our code and our style of development should be a main concern to all of us programmers. We should analyze ourselves and make sure we are using the proper style of development everywhere we do our work. Although the concept of style of development is not clearly defined, and it has its degree of subjectivity, it is very important.

I believe everyone will agree that our software applications and databases are influenced by our style of development. This is reflected especially in the area of performance because we are generally able to build a software application but at what cost? I am referring to the cost of development and to the cost of performance. All of this is influenced by our style of development.

I believe I have made my case. Some people will not be satisfied with my ideas, and that's their right. I respect the work of the application developer. I don't have a strong perspective of the user interface and application development, and I didn't evaluate their activity in their classic fields. I do, however, have a very good perspective of the relational database. I have a very good understanding of the SQL language. I have often been in the position of cleaning up code written by application developers in relational databases. This is why I strongly believe that the application developers need to make an effort to understand the concept of the data set and to follow set-oriented development inside the database. They need to write their code differently inside a relational database. I hope some application developers will understand and act accordingly.

With these final considerations I finish this book, and I hope you enjoyed it. I would be the happiest person in the world if at least one application developer learned something from my book or if some students started their first projects knowing that the database is something different. In addition, if anyone has earned the differences between the holistic and the atomic style of development, this would be another source of great satisfaction.

Index

■ T, U, V

■ W, X, Y, Z

Get the eBook for only $5!

Why limit yourself?

Now you can take the weightless companion with you wherever you go and access your content on your PC, phone, tablet, or reader.

Since you've purchased this print book, we're happy to offer you the eBook in all 3 formats for just $5.

Convenient and fully searchable, the PDF version enables you to easily find and copy code—or perform examples by quickly toggling between instructions and applications. The MOBI format is ideal for your Kindle, while the ePUB can be utilized on a variety of mobile devices.

To learn more, go to www.apress.com/companion or contact support@apress.com.

Printed in the United States
By Bookmasters